Sintra and ~~~~ Pena Palace
Regaleira
Belem
Tram
Tram ut

MAAT Gallery
Street Art Tour

Thomas Cook

LISBON & PORTO

BY
LOUISE POLE-BAKER

Produced by
Thomas Cook Publishing

Written by Louise Pole-Baker

Original photography by Neil Setchfield
and Luís Oliveira Santos

Editing and page layout by Cambridge
Publishing Management Limited,
149B Histon Road, Cambridge CB4 3JD

Published by Thomas Cook Publishing
A division of Thomas Cook UK Ltd

PO Box 227, The Thomas Cook Business Park, Units 19–21,
Coningsby Road, Peterborough PE3 8XX, United Kingdom
E-mail: books@thomascook.com
www.thomascookpublishing.com

ISBN: 1-841571-88-1

Text © 2003 Thomas Cook Publishing
Maps © 2003 Thomas Cook Publishing
First edition © 2003 Thomas Cook Publishing

Head of Publishing: Donald Greig
Project Editor: Charlotte Christensen
Project Administrator: Michelle Warrington
DTP: Steven Collins

Printed and bound in Spain by: Grafo Industrias Gráficas, Basauri

Cover: Lisbon Monument to the Discoveries, Portugal
Photograph by Gína Calvi/Alamy
Inside cover: photographs supplied by Spectrum Colour Library

CD manufacturing services provided by business interactive ltd, Rutland, UK
CD edited and designed by Laburnum Technologies PVT Ltd

Contents

Overview of Lisbon and Porto

A popular saying is that 'Lisbon plays, Braga prays and Porto works'. While it is not strictly true that Porto is all work and no play, or that Lisbon does no work, there are as many differences between the two cities as similarities.

The first problem to writing a guide about two cities is what to combine. There is a shared history on the one hand, a history that makes it one nation as opposed to several, but on the other hand, each place has historical differences. In the same way, social and cultural norms run throughout the country, but regional differences appear in food and lifestyle.

This opening section includes a couple of suggestions about acceptable social codes and the cost of living. This is followed by a general historical overview of the country which puts the local timelines into context, giving them clarity and linking them together into a whole.

The main section of the book concentrates on Lisbon and Porto themselves, with a historical overview and introduction to each city, followed by the main attractions. Finally, the directory has been placed in one section to facilitate quick access by the reader. Although there are differences, practical details remain more or less the same. Saying this, within each section of the directory, listings have been separated where relevant.

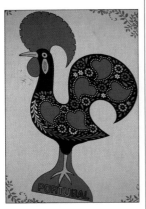

The cockerel has become a Portuguese national symbol

THE COST OF LIVING

Since Portugal became a member of the European Union, the standard and the cost of living have gone up. Even so, poverty still exists on levels not seen in most other countries in western Europe. Prices have also increased since the introduction of the Euro at the beginning of 2002. However, many things are still cheaper than in northern Europe, particularly clothes, entertainment and eating out, as well as housing. Visitors will also find that they can afford a better quality of accommodation than in most other places in western Europe. Even cheaper hotels and restaurants offer good quality and service.

The details are as accurate as possible, but while every effort has been made to keep the guide up to date, things can change overnight – bars and museums may move or change their opening hours, renovations may start and finish.

Manners and Mores

Throughout Portugal it is generally considered polite to say *bom dia* (good day), *boa tarde* (good evening), *boa noite* (good night), depending on the time of the day, but not *hola* (hello). Obviously the locals let it pass if a tourist is speaking but this is a general standard of formality, as is saying *obrigado/a* (thank you to a male and female respectively).

There are a couple of other useful things to keep in mind. Leaving a little food on the plate reflects the fact that you both enjoyed the food and have eaten sufficient. If you eat absolutely everything on your plate, they may think they have underserved you. However, Portuguese portions are ample and it is even acceptable in many places to share a main dish between two people.

It is not considered polite, however, to take your shoes off in public, whether under the table or in the park on a summer's day. In fact, Portuguese can find this quite disgusting, so stick with your sandals or shoes and leave the bare feet for the beach or the bathroom.

The Brasileira Café is renowned for its literary connections

Dom Afonso Henriques

History and Governance

Portugal has a history of occupation, from the Romans and Visigoths to the Moors and the Spanish; even the British have held sway over Portuguese Government and commerce. Today the country has a parliamentary democracy, but its independence and freedom has come at a price.

Initially Portugal developed separately from the rest of the Iberian peninsular due to geographic features that naturally separated it. This physical division led to the development of a socially distinct people and, eventually, an independent state.

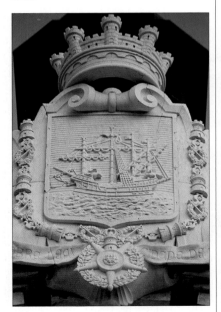

This coat of arms in Lisbon displays its maritime history

The Birth of the Portuguese Nation

The Moors occupied much of Portugal from AD 711, but by the 11th century the Reconquest was well underway. In 1128, Teresa in Guimarães wanted a union with Galicia but was defeated by her own son, Alfonso, near Guimarães. He then battled against his cousin Alfonso VII, but in 1139, declared himself the first King of Portugal after defeating the Moors in present-day Alentejo. Lisbon was secured in 1147, but the boundaries of the country were not finally secured until the end of the 13th century when Dom João I defeated the Castilians.

Maritime Explorations and the Economy

In the 14–16th centuries, Portuguese maritime explorations to find alternative routes for the spice trade led to a Golden Age of Discovery. With territory in Asia and Brazil, its monarchy became the richest in Europe, and Lisbon was the commercial capital of the world. However, this was more true on paper than in reality, and Portugal suffered. During the 16th and 17th centuries, bad economic management led to a decline. Manufactured goods were imported, and the persecution and expulsion of Jews, who were traditionally the educated ones, meant the country lacked in vital skills.

Spanish Rule and the Wars of Restoration

When Portugal's Cardinal king, Henrique, died in 1580 without leaving an heir, Phillip II of Spain became Felipe I of Portugal. The country lost territory to the Dutch and English under Spanish rule and Portuguese resentment grew. Eventually a group of noblemen lay siege to Lisbon in 1640 in what was called the Wars of Restoration and the Duke of Bragança was declared king, although Spain did not recognise Portuguese Independence until 1668.

Absolutism and the Birth of Modern Portugal

With the discovery of gold in Brazil at the end of the 17th century, an absolutist monarchy squandered money on luxurious palaces and churches, and when the Lisbon Great Earthquake took place in 1755, the country was still living under a medieval feudal system. The British also had a firm hand in its commerce, particularly in Porto's wine trade. It took the 'enlightened despot'

The Castelo de São Jorge crowns Lisbon's Alfama district

Marquês de Pombal (*see pp54–5*) to pull the country into shape with the set up of commercial monopolies, restrictions on British trade, the shake up of the education system and the rebuilding of Lisbon.

From Peninsular War to Portuguese Revolution

In the early 19th century, Portugal was pulled into the Peninsular War when Napoleonic troops invaded in 1807, and the royal family fled to Brazil for safekeeping. In 1811, the Duke of Wellington drove troops out again but constant war had left the country impoverished. In addition, the British were given direct access to trade with Brazil. Ten years later, in 1820, the Portuguese Revolution broke out. Dom João VI returned the following year and in 1822 Brazil broke away. Civil war and turbulence in Portugal remained for the next three decades.

Republicanism to Dictatorship

In the second half of the 19th century, Portugal saw some industrial growth, but it only managed to claim Angola and Mozambique in the scramble for Africa. Confidence in the monarchy slumped and Republicanism grew, culminating in the assassination of the king, Dom Carlos in 1908 and the assumption of control by the intelligentsia in 1910.

Portugal's problems were not over and it was pressurised into joining World War I by the British, destroying Republican plans and leaving it bankrupt. A *coup d'état* by Catholic army officers took place in 1926 and the economy was put in the hands of technocrat António Salazar (*see* p9), who soon became prime minister and ruled a repressive government for nearly 40 years.

Revolution and Parliamentary Democracy

The new ruling elite looked towards fascist politics in Italy and Germany and became increasingly austere during the great depression of the 1930s, while attempting to make money from the African colonies. Portugal became involved in World War II in 1943 by providing military bases in the Azores to the British and its allies. By the 1960s there was unrest in Mozambique and Angola and underground opposition was rising, leading to the bloodless Carnation Revolution in 1974. Afterwards, there was a surge in Marxist politics, the reading of previously censored publications and summer parties organised by the Communist Party. However, despite the initial euphoria, instability remained and another *coup d'état* took place in 1975.

Over the next ten years moderates controlled government, but the oil crisis in 1979 impeded any real growth and Portugal remained one of the poorest countries in Europe. Only after it joined the European Union in 1986 did it see any change in infrastructure and industry. Portugal now enjoys a parliamentary democracy, but behind it the class system and its system of favours still persist, along with higher rates of poverty than northern Europe. However, Portugal has moved into the new millennium with an increased rate of modernisation underway and the hope of returning to a golden age of prosperity.

António de Oliveira Salazar (1889–1970)

Born close to Viseu to a poor peasant Catholic family, António Salazar started out training as a priest but in 1910 went to the famous university of Coimbra to study law instead. This led into an academic career, which he pursued until he was persuaded to join the government of the First Republic following the coup of 1926. Although he was at first Minister of Finance, his position soon became powerful, and he swiftly moved into policy making. Eventually, in 1932, he became president of the council and founded the *Estado Novo*. His dictatorial control over the country continued until 1968, when he became too ill to continue. His politics were ultra-conservative and authoritarian. He repressed liberal thought and any opposition by banning strikes, censoring the press and by more extreme means. However, in the 1960s, pressures in the colonies and from the United Nations forced policy change and an end to the country's colonial empire.

Pavilhão Atlântico, Parque das Nações: one of the emblematic buildings of cultural modernity in Lisbon

Lisbon: Introduction

Sometimes referred to as the 'city of seven hills' and known for the nostalgic sound of its fado, Lisbon is a romantic place with a mixture of old winding streets and creaky trams. It has a wealth of history mixed in with its new modern outlook.

The Cristo Rei statue looks over Lisbon from the south side of the Rio Tejo

As with many cities in Europe, Lisbon started out as Roman and was referred to as *Felicitus Julia*. After a period of Roman fortification and road building, as well as the influence of the language, the city was taken by the Moors during invasions in the 8th century. The Moors built houses in the ancient district of al-Hamma (Alfama) and the city remained in their control until Dom Afonso Henriques (Afonso I) recaptured it in 1147 with the help of Crusaders.

He built the Sé Catedral and from here on Lisbon developed, both as a trading post and an administrative centre, finally replacing Coimbra as the capital of the country in 1260.

Lisbon had a period of glorious construction during the 15th century when the Age of Discoveries brought in knowledge and money from overseas. On the orders King Manuel I, the Mosteiro dos Jerónimos and the Torre de Belém, along with other buildings,

were constructed in the new *Manuelino* style of sumptuous architecture that reflects the exotic images from overseas, along with symbols of seafaring and heraldry.

Draining of funds by an absolutist and extravagant monarchy and the 60-year rule by the Spanish, depleted the capital, and the great earthquake of 1755 both destroyed and saved it. Under the eye of the Marquês de Pombal, the city was reconstructed and redirected, pulling it out of the medieval era into the Age of Enlightenment. This upset both the clergy and the nobility in the process, as their powers were curbed and their position in society changed.

Lisbon was rebuilt but suffered under Napoleonic invasions and subsequent civil war. By the early 20th century, the country had a republic but mismanagement led to a *coup*, and the 48-year dictatorship that followed stifled Lisbon and its cultural and social development. This finally came to an end in 1974 when rebel soldiers came out on to the streets of the city in the peaceful Carnation Revolution.

During the transition to democracy, Lisbon struggled with development but infrastructure began to improve after joining the European Union in 1986. In 1994, the city was designated European City of Culture, boosting its cultural output and tourism in the city, and in 1988, it saw the construction of the massive Cento Cultural de Belém (CCB). In 1998, the city hosted Expo '98, leading to the construction of the ultra-modern Parque das Nações and Vasco da Gama Bridge. Not only did the event attract people from all over the world to gaze at its city and learn about its glorious seafaring past, but it gave Lisbon a chance to show its modern side and its willingness to move forward.

Built on seven hills, there are numerous fabulous views of the city

background

Lisbon: City

Lisbon lies 38°42' north and 9° west at the mouth of the River Tagus (Tejo), which spills out into the Atlantic Ocean. The city population of almost 560,000 lives in an area of 84km² (32.5 sq miles), while the metropolitan area of Lisbon stretches to 2,750km² (1,062 sq miles) with a population of 2.1 million people.

Lisbon's dockside has become very trendy

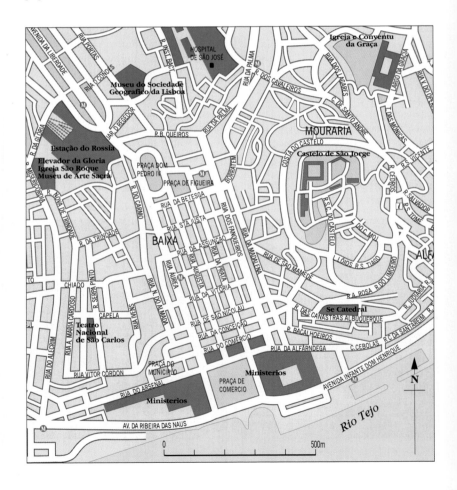

Lisbon is Portugal's capital and the country's largest city. Occupied by both the Romans and the Moors, it was won back again in the 12th century, became the capital in the 13th century and the focal point for the famous Golden Age of Discoveries, specifically Belém in the 16th and 17th centuries. The benefits of these conquests and expeditions were taken up by the monarchy and nobility, reflected in the level of construction of palaces and monuments at this time.

Like Rome and Prague, Lisbon is built on seven hills: Castelo, Graça, Monte, Penha de França, São Pedro de Alcântara, Santa Catarina and Estrela.

Rebuilt in the 18th century, following a devastating earthquake, the centre of Lisbon is now a medley of architectural styles and has spread in all directions, most recently with the development of the Parque das Nações following the hosting of Expo '98.

In the 20th century, the expansion of the city and the need for better transport and communication led to the construction of an airport, motorways, railways and two bridges: the Ponte 25 de Abril (built in 1966 and originally called the Ponte de Salazar after the dictator, the bridge's name was changed as a homage to the Carnation Revolution of 1974) and the Ponte Vasco da Gama (named after the city's best-known seafarer).

Areas of Lisbon

Lisbon has 53 parishes but is more commonly known by the names of its *bairros*, or neighbourhoods.

At the centre of the city on the edge of the River Tagus lies the Alfama, one of the oldest and most traditional neighbourhoods in the city, with the Castelo de São Jorge sitting on the top of the hill barely touched by the Great Earthquake of 1755. North of this lie the areas of Mouraria and Graça.

Just west of Alfama is the famous tourist district of Baixa, completely redesigned after the earthquake of 1755 and easy to navigate from the riverside

The Alfama is Lisbon's oldest and most traditional district

Praça do Comércio north to the Rossio and Restauradores Squares. From here a wide avenue, the Avenida da Liberdade, one of the city's main arteries, runs north with Rato and Amoreiras on the west side and Anjos on the east, before arriving at the Praça Marquês de Pombal, the very centre of the city. West of the Baixa are the old arty districts of the Chiado and the Bairro Alto and on to Madragoa and Estrela.

Together all these areas form the heart of the old city, which is of most interest to the tourist. The rest of the city radiates outwards from here, as do the transport systems.

A main road runs along the riverside. To the west, it reaches the monuments and palaces of Belém and on to the resort town of Estoril, passing the newly developed dockside restaurants and clubs of Alcântara on the way, as well as the 25 de Abril Bridge. To the east and northeast it goes up to the modern development of Parque das Nações and the new Vasco da Gama Bridge.

From the Praça Marquês de Pombal, the roads radiate out in five different directions. First, Rua Braamcamp to Rato, Estrela and down to Alcântara on the river. Second, Rua Joaquim António de Aguiar becomes the Avenida Engenheiro Duarte Pacheco and then connects up to the motorway network west to Estoril, south to Setúbal and northwest to Sintra. Third, the Avenida Fontes Pereira leads to Saldanha and Campo Pequena and in the direction of the airport and the motorway to Fatima to the north. Fourth, Avenida Duque de Loulé leads to the neighbourhood of Estefania. Finally, the Avenida da Liberdade runs south from Pombal to the Praça dos Restauradores

Climate

While Lisbon's climate is affected by its location on the River Tagus close to the Atlantic, its southerly position gives it more of a Mediterranean feel. In summer (May–September), the average temperature hovers just under 21°C but it can get much hotter than this. There is respite from the river and the seafront and the easy escape to nearby resorts. Although the average winter

Tiled panels (*azulejos*) can be seen on many buildings

Praça D Pedro IV, better known as Rossio Square

temperature is around 10.5°C, there can be a mixture of rainy days and bright blue sky, sometimes changing from T-shirt weather to the need for an umbrella several times in one day.

Marquês de Pombal

Sebastião José Carvalho e Melo (1699–1782), who later became the Marquês de Pombal, was one of the most influential figures in the history of modern Lisbon. While spending a period as ambassador to Great Britain, he picked up new ideas of equality and rationalism from academic circles. Under the incompetent Dom João I, who followed in the footsteps of his absolutist father, Pombal became one of three ministers who administered power. An opportunist and a man of action, Pombal used the earthquake to consolidate his absolute power. He achieved this efficiently and quickly.

He also imposed protectionist economic policies, empowering mercantile classes, and sought to impose many other reforms, making enemies of both the church and the nobility in the process. Pombal's redesign of the Baixa upset the nobility, and the expulsion of the Jesuits from all Portuguese dominions in 1759 led to state-controlled education. He introduced maths and philosophy and placed an increased emphasis on the sciences.

History

3rd century BC	The Romans proclaim Lisbon a municipality, giving it the name of *Felicitus Julia*, later calling it Olisippo. They provide the basis for the Portuguese language and start road building and fortification of the city.
AD 711	The Moors win Gibraltar. In AD 714, they arrive in Lisbon, now known as Lixbuna and other variations, and start building houses in al-Hamma (Alfama).
1147	Dom Afonso Henriques (Afonso I) recaptures Lisbon.
1260	Lisbon becomes the capital of the country under the reign of Dom Afonso III.
1386	The Treaty of Windsor tightens the ties of friendship with England. A year later the king marries Philippa of Lancaster and their third son is known as Prince Henry the Navigator.
15th century	Population rises to 50,000.
1479	Cristóbal Colón establishes himself in the city but eventually turns to Spain when the Portuguese monarchy refuses to finance his trip to the Indies.
1487	Bartolomeu Días leaves for the extreme south of Africa, sent on a mission by Dom João II.
1495	Dom Manuel I accedes to the throne. During his reign some of the most important discoveries are made. In addition, the most notable monuments in Lisbon are constructed and their style takes his name, *Manuelino*.
1497	Vasco da Gama leaves for India, starting from Belém and travelling round the Cape of Good Hope.
1501	Work starts on the Mosteiro dos Jerónimos.
1506	Around 2,000 people of Jewish ancestry are massacred.
1515–21	The Torre de Belém is built on the banks of the River Tagus.
1540	The first *auto-da-fé* takes place in Lisbon, which meant public execution for the 'converted' Jewish population.

1580	Phillip II of Spain takes over as Felipe I of Portugal after the country is left without an heir.
1640	In the War of Restoration, the palace is taken in Lisbon, and Portugal wins independence from Spain. The Duke of Bragança is subsequently crowned Dom João IV.
1755	A devastating earthquake destroys much of central Lisbon and its population. The city is rebuilt by the Marquês de Pombal.
1807	Napoleonic troops occupy Lisbon and the Portuguese royal family flee to Brazil. A year later the city is won back by the Duke of Wellington, but Dom João IV does not return until 1821.
1910	Dom Manuel II is deposed and the Republic is born.
1928	Dr António de Oliveira Salazar becomes finance minister and prime minister in 1932. He imposes the repressive *Estado Novo* until 1968.
1950	The first line on the metro network opens in Lisbon.

1960	The Monumento dos Descobrimentos (Discoveries Monument) is built in Belém to mark the 500th anniversary of the death of Henry the Navigator.
1966	The 25 de Abril Bridge is opened under the name of the Ponte Salazar.
1974	On 25 April, soldiers lead a bloodless revolution, known as the Carnation Revolution that ends the 48-year dictatorship.
1994	Lisbon is European City of Culture, injecting new confidence in the city.
1998	Lisbon hosts Expo '98, placing it firmly in the future with the construction of the Parque das Nações and the Vasco da Gama Bridge in the northeast of the city.

Statue of D João I,
Praça da Figueira

The *Revolução dos Cravos,* or Carnation Revolution, is the non-violent *coup d'état* that ended 48 years of dictatorship by prime minister António de Oliveira Salazar (and Marcelo Caetano, his successor) and eventually led to democracy in 1976. Driven by the lack of freedom, censorship, a repressive regime, poverty and colonial wars, the actions of a group of soldiers, backed by the population in general, also led to the freeing of numerous political prisoners, freedom of speech and independence to the colonies.

The roots of the revolt are complex, but basically mass poverty and shortages, along with civil war in various African colonies, led to unrest at home. Inspired by the assertion by general António de Spínola that self-rule in the colonies would be better, a few hundred army officers, who formed the Movimento das Forças Armadas (MFA, Armed Forces Movement) led by Francisco da Costa Gomes and Otelo Saraiva do Carvalho, organised the peaceful overthrow of the government.

The start of the Revolution was signalled by the radio broadcast at

12.25am on 25 April 1974 of the banned protest song 'Grândola, Vila Morena' by José Afonso. Taking the dictatorship by surprise, the soldiers entered the streets of Lisbon with red carnations protruding from their tanks and rifles, an image that became an icon of 1970s' Portugal. As people realised what was happening, they came on to the streets victoriously, standing on tanks, hugging and kissing, emerging from half a century of repression.

The Revolution succeeded in ridding the country of its dictatorship and gave the people a new lease of life and freedom, allowing them to read and listen to what they liked, leading to summer parties by the Communist Party.

However, the initial euphoria did not end the country's problems. The soldiers were unable to achieve stability and unrest continued for the next two years (and for much longer in the colonies), resulting in another *coup* in Portugal in November 1975.

This was the final turning point that brought about parliamentary democracy and allowed the start of the long struggle to rebuild the country. Real economic expansion did not take place until Portugal joined the European Union in 1986.

Facing page: Memorial to the Carnation Revolution in Parque Eduardo VII, Lisbon
Above: Soldiers placed carnations in their rifles as an act of defiance

Culture and Festivals in Lisbon

Located on the western edge of Europe, for a long time Lisbon has looked hopefully out on the Atlantic, remembering a glorious past. Now very much part of Europe, a new kind of cultural exploration is taking place. While much of its cultural output is still very Portuguese, its cultural influence is growing and gaining recognition internationally.

Torre de Belém

Art and Architecture

Lisbon's history is reflected through its art and architecture. Moorish elements barely remain in the city's oldest district of Alfama, with remnants of walls almost buried under the Christian forces

The Museu Gulbenkian houses an eclectic collection of artefacts

that crushed them, and the reclaimed Castelo de São Jorge looking over the city to ensure its protection.

The Reconquest led to the building of Gothic churches such as the Sé Catedral. However, it was the wealth brought in by the Age of Discoveries in the 15th and 16th centuries that led to increased construction and the emergence of a Portuguese architecture, *Manuelino* or Manueline (*see pp32–3*). This can be seen in the heraldic, seafaring and exotic motifs of the Mosteiro dos Jerónimos and the Torre de Belém. Palaces were also built in Belém and the Paço de Terreiro, now the Praça de Comércio. Most of the new buildings were built by the monarchy, church and nobility, while the rest of the population lived in the old medieval buildings.

Unfortunately, all the fortresses in the world could not protect the city from natural destruction. Some of the excesses of the nobility were crushed by the Great Earthquake of 1755 and washed away by the tidal wave that followed. Subsequently, the centre of the city, particularly the Baixa, was recreated

The Tivoli is one of the more 'traditional' cinemas

by the Marquês de Pombal in the spirit of the Age of Enlightenment.

The functionality of the Baixa led to the emergence of a neo-classical middle-class neighbourhood of merchants and traders. During the 18th and 19th centuries this area was extended by the Avenida da Liberdade, a symbol of modernity, and luxurious mansions were built along it.

Also at this time many theatres were built, such as the Teatro Nacional Dona Maria II in Rossio and the Teatro Nacional de São Carlos in the Chiado, which replaced the old opera house destroyed in the Great Earthquake.

Apart from the Ponte 25 de Abril and some beautiful Art Deco buildings such as the Orion Eden hotel, cultural output was stifled by an oppressive dictatorship for 48 years during the 20th century. Towards the end of the dictatorship, the country's most important cultural institution, the Gulbenkian Foundation, began, but it was not until the 1980s that Lisbon really started to look forward once more.

Rising urbanisation led to new residential areas and the expansion of the city and increased spending power led to the construction of ultra-modern shopping centres such as Amoreiras and the huge Colombo. New cultural centres also emerged, for instance the Centro Cultural de Belém and the Museu do Chiado. With the hosting of Expo '98, a whole new modern area, the Parque das Nações and the Ponte Vasco da Gama, placed Lisbon firmly in the modern architectural marketplace.

Art in Lisbon has developed alongside its architecture. The *azulejos* hand-painted ceramic tiles are both part of the decoration of the building and reflect the historical and economic situation (*see pp114–15*) as well as the artistic movements. This process continues today, especially in Lisbon's metro system.

Portuguese painters from the 15th century, such as Nuno Gonçalves and Grão Vasco, produced works that portrayed the Age of Discoveries. Religion was also at the forefront of painting at this time, while other artists worked on royal portraits, including Jorge Afonso and Cristóvão de Morais.

The 18th and 19th centuries also saw renowned artists, such as Domingos António de Sequeiros from Belém and Alfredo Keil.

In the 20th century, leading artists included Júlio Pomar, Mário Cesarinhy, Maria Helena Vieira da Silva and Paula Rego, while today more contemporary artists include António Carmo, who is one of the best-known Portuguese painters.

Lisbon is renowned for its Fado musicians

Music

Lisbon is renowned for its fado, the nostalgic music heard throughout the Bairro Alto and Alfama, and this sound became internationalised with singers such as Amália Rodrigues and Carlos do Carmo. It developed further with groups like Madredeus and the singer Dulce Pontes. However, today there is more than fado to be heard in Lisbon.

In the past few decades, the city has produced several jazz musicians, such as Maria João and Mário Laginha. Many more have emerged due to the city's now-legendary 'jazz cave' and school, the Hot Clube, including Carlos Barretto and Mário Barreiros.

Lisbon also boasts the internationally renowned Gulbenkian Orchestra and Choir (*see pp46–7*) and the Teatro Nacional de São Carlos orchestra.

Literature and Drama

Numerous writers have been associated with Lisbon over the centuries and the most notable include:

- **Luís de Camões**, who completed his most outstanding work *Os Lusíadas* in 1572 and is associated with the Discoveries;
- The 19th-century poet **António Ribeiro**;
- **José Maria Eça de Queiros** (1846–1900) who set his book *To the Capital* (1925) in Lisbon;
- **Fernando Pessoa**, considered the most important modern writer in Portugal (*see pp62–3*) who based much of his work around the capital;
- Contemporary writer **Jose Saramago** has also set works in Lisbon, including *The Year of the Death of Ricardo Reis*

(1984) and *The History of the Siege of Lisbon* (1989);

- Although he is not Portuguese, **Richard Zimler's** work, *The Last Kabbalist of Lisbon* (1998), illuminates a horrific period of Lisbon's history, the massacre of Jews in 1506, based on a 16th-century manuscript by a Portuguese Jewish exile.

Festivals in Lisbon

Within Portugal, Lisbon is known as the city that likes to party, closing every year and starting the new with a massive party in Belém. The **Noite Mágica**, as it is called, sees thousands of people converge on the area to listen to bands and dance until the early hours. The other big annual event takes place during June with the **Lisbon Festivities**, celebrating the feast of St Anthony, who was born here. From 12–30 June the centre of the city is overtaken by all kinds of musical performances and fireworks.

Other annual festivals include:

- The **Centro Cultural de Belém Music Festival** in April, each year dedicated to a different theme;
- Portugal's **National Day**;
- The renowned **Sintra Music Festival** with performances by major international orchestras;
- **Baixanima**, a popular and traditional free arts festival throughout the summer in the Baixa/Chiado district;
- The summer **Estoril Jazz Festival** at the famous resort along the coast, with plenty of top names;
- **Sintra Ballet Festival** in July and August, featuring events throughout the World Heritage Site;

- **Jazz at the Gulbenkian**, open-air concerts in August in the beautiful gardens of the Gulbenkian Foundation;
- October's **ModaLisboa**, where Portugal's top designers show their latest collections;
- Sports fans might also be interested in noting that Lisbon hosts an annual **marathon** every December and a **half-marathon** in March.

Tiled panels (*azulejos*) reflect cultural life too

Impressions

The airport is close to the city and you can be in the heart of Lisbon within 30 minutes of your arrival. The swift drive is along wide avenues, passing a mixture of modern and traditional architecture. Once you have found your feet, it is difficult not to notice that Lisbon is built on several hills, seven to be precise, and that you need your walking legs to discover its gems of history and culture.

25 de Abril Bridge

Lisbon is packed with stories waiting to be discovered by each new visitor. The district of Alfama is a tangle of ancient streets with a history of Moorish invasions and a medieval castle, as well as fishmongers and markets, while the Bairro Alto is criss-crossed with literary connections, lively fado houses and cafés. Both look over the River Tagus and the grid-like structure of the Baixa, once the 'modern' part of town when it was built following the Great Earthquake in 1755.

As you walk up and down through the streets, you see old mansions and palaces, churches and tiles, gardens and parks and beautiful belvederes with views over the city. Further west, the contrasting area of Belém is a mishmash of styles from the *Manuelino* masterpieces to the modern cultural centre, displaying its nautical past of discovery and adventure, and its move into the future.

Dotted around the city, shopping malls have sprung up in the past 10– 20 years, bringing international styles ranging from fashion to cars and multiplex cinemas. The northeast of Lisbon firmly displays this modernisation with the singularly modern complex of the Parque das Nações. Lisbon remains a place to relax, to have a coffee and take the family out for a stroll, very much a city and without the hard edge of other capitals.

When to Go

Although Lisbon can get very hot in the summer, there is some respite due to the fact that it lies on the edge of the River Tagus. Many people escape to the beach resorts west and south of the city at this time, where you can cool off in the ocean. The best times to go are spring and autumn when it can still be T-shirt weather and, although the winters are never unbearably cold, you will need a jacket. Rainfall is much higher from October to February, so take an umbrella or raincoat.

Getting Around

Although many places in Lisbon are best seen on foot, it is impossible to get from one side of the city to the other without taking some form of transport. The public transport system is cheap and efficient as well as easy to follow. City maps are available from the tourist

The Praça do Comércio is a good starting point for seeing the city

office and good bookshops. The tourist office will also give you information on the transport system, tours and the nearest place to buy passes.

Tram

In the past few decades, many tramlines have been taken out of service. However, there are still several running in areas without metro lines, notably the Alfama and Belém, and through Estrela. No 28 runs through the scenic areas from Campo Ourique, Estrela, the Bairro Alto, Baixa and on to Alfama and Graça, but it is well known that tourists take this tram more than the others and you should watch out for pickpockets.

Most of the trams are antiquated, and perhaps that is part of the charm, but there are also newer 'double' trams, such as the No 15 that runs from Praça do Comércio to Algés more or less along the riverfront through Belém. Tickets can be bought at the machines on board or you can get passes for one day or longer that can also be used on the buses and elevators. There are inspectors checking from time to time, so make sure you have a ticket or you will have to pay an on-the-spot fine.

Metro

The metro is clean and safe and runs everywhere except the southwest of the city and the very northern part. New stations have been constructed in the past few years running up to Oriente station in the Parque das Nações, and further stations are being built from Baixa Chiado to Santa Apolónia Station.

You can buy single tickets or passes for one day or longer at the counter or at a machine in the station.

Buses

Lisbon has a good bus network both in the centre and to outlying areas. The buses are frequent and useful for getting to parts of the city where there are no metro stations. There are also night buses from Cais do Sodré that run through the main arteries of the city every 30 minutes. You can get passes for one day or more that also work on the trams and elevators.

Elevators

There are four lifts/elevators in the city which date back to the late 19th century and are still useful for getting up Lisbon's steep hills. The most famous are the Elevador da Glória, which runs from Restauradores to the Bairro Alto, and the Elevador de Santa Justa, from the Baixa to the Bairro Alto. However, due to safety problems the exit to the Bairro Alto has been suspended and you can only go to the viewing platform and restaurant at the top. The other two elevators, the Ascensor do Lavra and the Ascensor da Bica, run from Rua Câmara Pestana to Largo da Anunciada (east of Avenida da Liberdade), and from Largo do Calhariz to Rua de São Paulo (Chiado) respectively.

Taxis

There are plenty of taxis and you should have no problem hailing one in the street or waiting at a taxi rank. They are

Rest those feet and take the Elevador da Glória from Restauradores to the Bairro Alto

There are plenty of comfortable local and national trains

reasonably priced and run on a meter. Taxi drivers often ask if you require a receipt, but you can request one if they do not ask. If you want a taxi from the airport you have to go to the tourist office desk (Lisbon Welcome Centre) in Arrivals for a voucher.

Car

The transport system in Lisbon is so efficient that driving is not the most practical form of getting around the central part of the city. Areas such as the Bairro Alto and Estrela have narrow streets that become clogged with traffic, and the Alfama's streets are so narrow you can barely get a car along many of them. As you move away from these areas, there are more wide avenues and plenty of underground car parks, particularly at the shopping malls. However, Portuguese driving can be somewhat erratic, so hiring or taking your own car is not for the faint-hearted.

Pollution in Lisbon

The coastal waters in the area around Lisbon suffer in the summer due to tourism. As well as the increase in human waste, industrial waste along the Atlantic coast and in the River Tagus produces algae, which can be harmful to delicate flora and fauna. EU policy has to be adhered to and solutions are being pursued.

Museums

Lisbon is lucky to have two major cultural institutions, the Fundação Calouste Gulbenkian and the Centro Cultural de Belém. In addition, the city boasts numerous museums that cover everything from the arts to science and technology. The most important of these are the Museu Nacional de Arte Antiga and the Museu Nacional do Azulejo but do explore some of the smaller, specialist ones.

Looking up the steps of the Museo Nacional de Arte Antiga (the Green Shutter Museum)

The following list includes a selection of the most interesting museums for the visitor.

Museu Antoniano

The museum contains a small collection of iconography and other objects related to the worship of St Anthony, the patron Saint of Lisbon. It is located next to the church dedicated to him.
Largo de São António da Sé. Tel: 21 886 0447. Open: Tue–Sun 10am–1pm & 2–6pm. Closed public holidays. Admission charge.

Museu da Agua da Epal

The headquarters of the museum are housed in the Barbadinhos Steam Pumping Station, an example of 19th-century industrial architecture, and include a historical view of the city's water supply. Don't miss the **Aqueduto das Aguas Livres** and the reservoirs. The 18th-century aqueduct is considered one of the most remarkable examples of hydraulic engineering and was not touched by the famous Lisbon Great Earthquake of 1755.
Museum: *Rua Alviela, 12. Tel: 21 810 0215; www.epal.pt/. Open: Mon–Sat 10am–6pm. Closed public holidays. Admission charge. Buses: 9, 12, 25A, 28, 39, 46, 59, 81 & 82.*
Aqueduct: *Open: 1 Mar–31 Oct, Mon–Sat 10am–6pm. Closed public holidays. Admission charge. Buses: 2, 13 to Serafina, 2, 12 & 18 to Campolide.*
Reservatório da Patriarcal *(reservoir): Jardim do Príncipe Real. Open: Mon–Sat 10am–6pm. Closed public holidays. Admission charge. Buses: 58 & 100.*
Mãe-D'Agua das Amoreiras *(reservoir): Praça das Amoreiras, 10. Open: Mon–Sat 10am–6pm. Closed public holidays. Admission charge. Metro: Rato. Buses: 6, 9, 11, 20, 22, 23, 27, 48, 49, 53, 58 & 74.*

Museu da Cidade

Located in the Palácio Pimenta, a royal summer residence in the 18th century, the museum contains an impressive collection of *azulejos* panels from the era. There is

also a large art collection that tells the history of Lisbon from prehistoric times to the 19th century. A large model of the city shows what the city was like before the devastating Great Earthquake of 1755.
Campo Grande, 245. Tel: 21 751 3200. Open: Tue–Sun 10am–1pm & 2–6pm. Admission charge. Metro: Campo Grande. Buses: 1, 3, 7, 7A, 33, 36, 47, 50, 68, 85, 101 & 108.

Museu da Electricidade
Housed in the Central Tejo, Lisbon's power station, the building is as much of interest as the museum, which includes steam engines, dynamos and electric engines, hydraulic generators and other equipment.
Central Tejo, Avenida de Brasília. Tel: 21 363 1646. Closed until 2004, then open: Tue–Sun 10am–12.30pm & 2–5.30pm (May–Sept closes 8pm). Tram: 15. Buses: 14, 28, 43, 49 & 51.

Museu da Música
Contains a large collection of musical instruments , various documents and a sound archive.
Rua João de Freitas Branco. Tel: 21 355 8457. Open: Tue–Sat 1.30–8pm. Closed 1 Jan, 1 May & 25 Dec. Admission charge. Metro: Estação Alto dos Moinhos. Buses: 68 & 54.

Museu de Arte Popular
Portuguese folk art from all over the country from ceramics and furniture to filigree and basketwork.
Avenida Brasilia. Tel: 21 301 1675. Open: Tue–Sun 10am–12.30pm & 2–5pm. Admission charge. Tram: 15. Buses: 27, 28, 43, 49 & 51.

Museu de Marinha
Located in the north and west wings of the Mosteiro dos Jerónimos, the collection at the Maritime Museum has more than 17,000 items including several model ships from the 18th century.
Praça do Império. Tel: 21 362 0010. Open: Tue–Sun 10am–5pm (6pm in the summer). Closed public holidays. Admission charge. Tram: 15.

Museu do Chiado
The museum houses an impressive collection of paintings, sculptures and drawings from 1850–1960, including the most representative Portuguese artists from this period.
Rua Serpa Pinto, 4. Tel: 21 343 2148. Open: Wed–Sun 10am–6pm, Tue 2–6pm, Sun & public holidays 10am–2pm. Admission charge. Metro: Baixa-Chiado. Tram: 28. Buses: 58 & 100.

Museu das Artes Decorativas
Part of the Fundação Ricardo do Espírito Silva, it was founded by and named after a banker/art collector who donated the 17th-century Palácio de Azurara and his private collections to the Portuguese state.
Decorated in the style of an 18th-century aristocratic residence, the museum contains important Portuguese *azulejos* as well as furniture and textiles.
Largo das Portas do Sol, 2. Tel: 21 881 4600. Open: Tue–Sun 10am–5pm. Admission charge. Trams: 12 & 28. Bus: 37.

Museu Militar
The museum displays artillery, war relics and paintings dating back to the 15th century.

Watching guard at the Museu Nacional de Azulejo

Largo do Museu da Artilharia. Tel: 21 884 2569. Open: Tue–Sun 10am–5pm. Closed public holidays. Buses: 9, 12, 25, 28, 35, 39, 46, 104, 105 & 107.

Museu Nacional de Arqueologia

Founded in 1893 by Dr José Leite de Vasconcelos, the museum is housed in the monk's old quarters next to the Mosteiro dos Jerónimos. The collection includes architecture, ceramics, bronze artefacts, weapons, tools and mosaics, with pieces dating back as far as the Iron Age.

Praça do Império. Tel: 21 362 0000. Open: Tue 2–6pm, Wed–Sun 10am–6 pm. At some times of the year and for some temporary exhibitions the museum closes noon–2pm. Admission charge. Tram: 15.

Museu Nacional de Arte Antiga or Museu das Janelas Verdes

One of Portugal's most important museums, it is located in a 17th-century palace renowned for its green shutters, thus the nickname of the 'Green Shutter Museum'. The main focus is on the fantastic collection of work by Portuguese artists from the 15–19th centuries, as well as paintings by European artists. There are also stunning pieces of Portuguese and Oriental ceramics and decorative pieces, including Portugal's most important collection of gold and silverware.

Rua das Janelas Verdes. Tel: 21 391 2800. Open: Wed–Sun 10am–6pm, Tue 2–6pm. Closed 1 Jan, Easter Sunday, 1 May and 25 Dec. Admission charge. Trams: 15 & 18. Buses: 27, 40, 49 & 60.

Museu Nacional do Azulejo

Housed in a former 16th-century Madre de Deus convent, the museum holds one of the most important collections of ceramic tiles in the world. The collection follows the development of Portugal's *azulejos* from the 15th century to the present.

Rua da Madre de Deus, 4. Tel: 21 814 7747. Open: Wed–Sun 10am–6pm, Tue 2–6pm. Closed 1 Jan, Good Friday, Easter Sunday, 1 May & 25 Dec. Admission charge. Buses: 18, 42, 104 & 105.

Museu Nacional do Teatro

Located inside the Palácio do Monteiro-Mor, an 18th-century residence with a beautiful park, the museum exhibits costumes, props and theatrical set designs.

Estrada do Lumiar, 12. Tel: 21 757 0318.
Open: Wed–Sun 10am–6pm, Tue 2–6pm,
Closed public holidays. Admission charge.
Buses: 1, 3, 7, 36, 101 & 108.

Museu Nacional do Traje

Also located in the Palácio do Monteiro-
Mor, the museum hosts exhibitions of
traditional and historical costumes,
mainly from the 18th century.
Largo Júlio de Castilho. Tel: 21 759 0318.
Open: Tue–Sun 10am–6pm. Closed public
holidays. Admission charge.
Buses: 1, 3, 7, 36, 101 & 106.

Museu Nacional dos Coches

Located in the former royal riding school,
the museum contains a unique collection
of coaches, articles related to
horsemanship and paintings of members
of the Royal House of Bragança.
Praça de Afonso de Alburquerque. Tel: 21
361 0850. Open: Tue–Sun 10am–6pm.
Admission charge. Tram: 15. Buses: 14,
27, 28, 29, 43, 49, 51 & 73.

Palácio dos Marqueses de Fronteira

This 17th-century palace has azulejos
from the period and 18th-century
stucco work as well as furniture and
formal gardens.
Largo S Domingos de Benfica, 1. Tel: 21
778 2023. Open: guided visits June–Sept,
10.30–11am & 11.30am–noon; Oct–May,
11am–noon.

Palácio Nacional da Ajuda

This 19th-century neo-classical palace
chosen as the residence for the
Portuguese royal family in the 19th
century became a museum in 1938.
It has an important collection of
decorative art and hosts some important
presidential ceremonies.
Largo da Ajuda. Tel: 21 363 7095.
Open: Thur–Tue 10am–5pm. Closed
1 Jan, Good Friday, Easter Sunday, 1 May
& 25 Dec. Admission charge. Tram: 18.
Buses: 14, 32, 42 & 60.

Museu Nacional dos Coches

Manuelino Architecture

Manuelino (or Manueline) architecture is Portugal's own unique national decoration style, dating back to the 16th century. Named after the king that ruled at the time – Dom Manuel I of Portugal (reigned 1495–1521) – today it stands as a monument to Portuguese culture and history.

Cloisters of the Mosteiro dos Jerónimos

Lasting around 50 years (1490–1540), the origins of the style lie in the voyages made by Portuguese navigators during the 15th century. Inspired by explorations of Africa and the discovery of routes to the Far East, architects incorporated sculptured organic features such as shells, exotic fruits and plants, rope, sails, twisted columns and even the letter 'M' (for Manuel) into their designs. They adorned porticos, windows, columns and archways – a shift from the old Gothic style to a more elaborate one.

Alongside the marine elements and representation of the voyages, each building combined symbols of power, heraldry and religion. One of the most important and prevalent of these was the armillary sphere and the *cruzes da Ordem Militar de Cristo* – crosses representing the military order that helped fund the early voyages, a symbol that often appeared on sails and flags at that time.

More than a pure reflection of Portugal's navigational successes, *Manuelino* was an assertion of Portuguese power and independence, and the rejection of Spanish attempts at domination during the previous century. Dom Manuel I commissioned numerous buildings to assert this new-found confidence and imperial prosperity.

Although *Manuelino* architecture can be found all over the mainland and Madeira and the Azores, the style is most prevalent in central Portugal. For a trip out of Lisbon, visit the first known example, the **Igreja de Jesus**. This was built in Setúbal in 1495 by French-born architect Diogo de Boitaca, who settled in Portugal and became the Mestre de Obras do Reino (Master of Royal Works).

In Lisbon you can see the country's best-known examples, also built by Boitaca – the **Torre de Belém**, built with Francisco de Arruda, and the **Mosteiro dos Jerónimos**, built with João de Castilho *et al.* Other Boitaca buildings can be found further away at the **Mosteiro de Batalha** (south of Coimbra) and the **Mosteiro de Santa Cruz de Coimbra**. Further renowned works include the **Palácio Real de Lisboa** and the **Convento de Cristo in Tomar** on the Costa da Prata, built by Diogo de Arruda. The window of the convent in Tomar is one of the most elaborate examples of the style.

Despite Portugal's anti-Spanish stance, it was influenced by the

The Mosteiro de Jerónimos is one of the major examples of Manueline architecture

Plateresque style (reminiscent of silverware) that emerged at the same time. *Manuelino* relief work was considered to be much more intricate and of higher artistic quality than the Plateresque, but over time more overseas influence was assimilated. With the cost of overseas colonies following the death of Manuel I, construction diminished and the *Manuelino* style faded away.

In the early 19th century, however, there was a rejuvenation of the Portuguese style, particularly in private homes. The **Palácio do Buçaco**, a luxury palace in the Beiras that formerly belonged to the Portuguese royal family, is a sumptuous show of the *Neomanuelino* style, while one of the most famous public buildings is Lisbon's **Rossio Station**.

The Torre de Belém displays typical regal, natural, maritime and religious symbolism

Salazar's Museum - amazing building →

Without a doubt, Portugal was at the forefront of Europe's Golden Age of Discovery, an era when maritime routes were mapped out and the world was carved up in the name of trade, labour, land and riches.

Three main figures stand out in Portugal's maritime history – Henry the Navigator (1394–1460), Vasco da Gama (1460–1524) and Fernão de Magalhães, known as Ferdinand Magellan (1480–1521) – but there were numerous attempts, failures and successes by various seafarers.

In 1415, the Infante Henrique, better known as Prince Henry the Navigator, was chosen to lead an expedition to the North African city of Ceuta, a Muslim stronghold. As Henry was a member of the religious Order of Christ, he was a crusader as well as a discoverer and this motivated him to search out the 'unconverted' followers of Islam. He started studying geography and developing navigation techniques, setting himself up in the southern Portuguese city of Sagres.

Henry sent various expeditions out but no one would go beyond Cape Bojador, south of the Canaries, until Gil Eanes in 1435. Eanes continued south 'beyond the end of the world' and started the African slave trade in 1444 with the capture of 200 people near Cape Blanco. Other expeditions took place to search out gold, known to be in abundance in West Africa. By the second half of the 15th century, some of the trade was diverted from the Gold Coast, controlled by the Portuguese monarchy.

This period also included the colonisation of various islands, most of which were sponsored by Henry the Navigator: the Canary Islands, later transferred to Castile; Madeira and the Azores; the Cape Verde islands and São Tomé. Crops were planted here, including vines, wheat, cotton, sugar cane and indigo dyes, attracting Portuguese settlers, a pattern that would continue in other colonisations.

Although Bartolomeu Dias passed round the Cape of Good Hope in 1487, it was Vasco da Gama who opened up the trade

route in 1498 after continuing on to Calicut in India. The market was finally forced open in 1502 and the spice trade brought considerable wealth to Portugal.

In 1500, Brazil was discovered by accident when João Cabral drifted too far west on an expedition to India and landed on the southern tip of the country. The Spanish had also started exploring with a successful voyage by Cristobal Colón (Christopher Columbus) to the 'New World'. Constantly in conflict with the Spanish, the Portuguese had a new battle on their hands as claims were made for new territories. Pope Alexander VI solved this with the Treaty of Tordesillas in 1494, which drew an imaginary line in the Atlantic 100 leagues west of the Cape Verde islands. Spain had claim to undiscovered territory west of here and Portugal to the east. So when Cabral landed in Brazil, he discovered what already belonged, according to the treaty, to the Portuguese.

Subsequent expeditions led to the colonisation and setting up of trading posts in Mozambique, Angola, Mombassa, Timor, China, Japan, Goa and Macau. Having power and maintaining their lead at the forefront of trade was all-important (as was the conversion of the indigenous peoples to Christianity).

The last main maritime figure in this golden age was Magellan, who led the first circumnavigation of the globe in 1519. Although Magellan was Portuguese, the king would not fund his seemingly frivolous journey, and Magellan turned to the Spanish, winning their backing with promises of proving that the coveted Spice Islands or Moluccas belonged to Spain. However, although he passed what are now called the Straits of Magellan on the southern tip of South America and sailed into the Pacific Ocean, starvation and cold drove his ship to the Philippines. The crew replenished themselves but, after trying to convert the population to Christianity, Magellan was killed.

The cost of the expeditions and the bleeding of income by the monarchy eventually led Portugal into decline. When Spain's Phillip II (Felipe I of Portugal) claimed the throne in 1580, the golden age came to an end.

Facing page: Vasco da Gama *et al* look out to the seas they sailed from the Padrão dos Descrobimentos
Above: Vasco da Gama's tomb lies inside the Mosteiro dos Jerónimos

Mosteiro dos Jerónimos (Jeronimos Monastery)

Constantly under the gaze of historians, visitors and artists, the Jeronimos Monastery in the heart of Belém is more than a beautiful piece of architecture. It is a symbol of Portuguese culture and identity, reflected in its status as a National Monument and a UNESCO World Heritage Site.

The south portal of the monastery is the most impressive

The monastery was originally built on the order of Dom Manuel I, who wanted a monastery at the entrance to Lisbon. Work started in 1501 and nearly a century of construction came under the direction of several architects, including *Manuelino* 'master' Diogo de Boitaca, João de Castilho, Diogo de Torralva and Jerónimo de Ruã, each adding their own artistic expression.

Commonly known as the 'Mosteiro dos Jerónimos', the monastery was actually dedicated to the Virgin of Belém and built on the grounds of a previous church dedicated to her. The name of Jerónimos comes from the order of monks that resided there and gave spiritual help to seafarers and navigators on their way to discover new worlds. The order stayed until 1833 when it was dissolved. The convent area of the monastery then housed students of the Casa Pia de Lisboa until around 1940.

With its 300m (984ft) long facade and highly decorated interior, the monastery is often referred to as the 'jewel' of *Manuelino* architecture. However, it underwent some architectural changes in the 19th century, particularly to the bell tower cupola, the dormitories (today the Museu de Arqueologia) and the chapter house. The most interesting parts of the monastery are the portals, the church, the cloisters and the refectory.

Portals

While the main portal is, in principle, the main entrance, the visual centrepiece of the monastery's facade is the south portal. Its focal point is a statue of Our Lady of Belém, surrounded by statues of prophets, apostles and virgin saints. The statue of the Archangel St Michael sits atop the portal, and there are also scenes from the life of São Jerónimo.

The smaller or main portal, located to the left, depicts scenes from the birth of Christ. On either side of the portal are statues of the founding king and queen, Dom Manuel I and Dom Maria, with their patron saints, São Jerónimo and São João Baptista respectively.

Church of Santa Maria

Designed in the shape of a cross, the church has three naves of the same height. The fan-vaulted ceiling was one of the most ambitious constructions of the late medieval period with the largest space possible supported by just six columns. The church contains the tombs of Vasco da Gama on the right and Luís de Camões on the left, both carved in the 19th century by sculptor Costa Mota.

At the east end of the church is the main chapel, built on the order of Dom Catarina, the wife of Dom João III, in 1571. The most interesting feature to note is that it was built in the Mannerist style, completely contrasting with the *Manuelino* style of the church. You can see the tomb of Dom Manuel I and other members of his family, and religious paintings by Lourenço de Salzedo (produced 1572–4).

Cloisters

Intended mainly to isolate the monastic community from the public, this was a serene space for the praying and meditation of the monks. Two storeys high around a quadrangle, it is one of the most significant examples of *Manuelino* architecture with religious, regal and natural symbolism. Recent renovations have brought back their stunning beauty. On the north side is the tomb of poet Fernando Pessoa (*see pp62–3*), laid there in 1985.

Refectory

This was built by Leonard Vaz and his artisans from 1517–18. Today the base of the stone walls are covered in panels of *azulejos,* which date from 1780–5 and depict scenes from the Old and New Testament. At one end there is a wooden pulpit, where the scriptures and lives of the saints were read during meals. *Tel: 21 362 0034. Open: Oct–April, Tue–Sun 10am–5pm; May–Sept, 10am–6.30pm. Closed 1 Jan, Easter Sunday, 1 May & 25 Dec. Admission charge. Tram: 15. Trains: Cascais line from Belém. Buses: 27, 28, 29, 43, 49, 51 & 112.*

The monastery's cloisters have been renovated to their former stunning glory

Walk: Belém

This walk takes you to the main historical sites in Belém. However, with so many museums and cultural sites it is worthwhile spending more than a couple of hours there.
Allow 3 hours at least. Begin at the Praça Afonso de Albuquerque. Tram No 15 takes you there from the Praça do Comércio.

1 Monumento a Afonso de Albuquerque (Monument)
At the centre of the square is a monument dedicated to Afonso de Albuquerque (1462–1515), first viceroy of India. The *neomanuelino* monument has Afonso on top with rope-like columns, four angels at the bottom and maritime images between them. On the base of the statue you can see scenes from his life.
Cross the square to Rúa de Belém.

2 Palácio Nacional de Belém
The pink palace was built in 1559 and it used to be a royal summer residence with gardens on the banks of the River Tagus (before it receded). Today it is the official residence of the President of Portugal. The palace and the beautiful old palace gardens on Calçada do Galvão can be visited by prior arrangement (*tel: 21 361 4660*).
Continue left along Rúa de Belém, stopping off at the famous Pasteis de Belém cake shop. Continue along the road and cross over the Largo dos Jerónimos.

3 Mosteiro dos Jerónimos
Here you will see the Mosteiro dos Jerónimos (*see pp36–7*). Built in the 16th century on the order of Dom Manuel I, it has some of the best examples of *Manuelino* architecture (*see pp32–3*) and the old refectory has some good *azulejos*.
Walk along the length of the Mosteiro. At the end on the right-hand side you will see the Museu da Marinha and the Planétario Gulbenkian. On the left there is the modern structure of the Centro Cultural de Belém (see pp40–1). Cross over at the crossing and you can walk through the centre along a pathway.

4 Centro Cultural de Belém (CCB)
You can stop at the museums, cafés, restaurants or terraces that overlook the river.
Praça do Império 1400. Tel: 21 361 2400. At the end of the pathway turn right along Avenida da India and cross the pedestrian bridge to the park. Continue along the pathway veering to the right.

5 Torre de Belém
Classified in 1983 as a World Heritage Site, this is a symbol of Portugal's maritime exploits as well as one of the best examples of *Manuelino* architecture – note the stone ropes around it, the heraldic motifs and the famous carving

Pop in for a *pastel* (cake) at the famous Belém Pasteis Café

of a rhinoceros. Built from 1514–20 by Francisco de Arruda, it has a quadrangular tower with a watchtower at each corner. The most decorated part is the balcony with its latticework balustrade and royal coat of arms above. Although it is hard work walking up all the steps, it is worth it for the views of the river and the city alone.

Praça do Império 1400. Tel: 21 361 2400. Come out of the tower and walk along the river towards the Ponte 25 de Abril in the distance. Continue along the river to the Discoveries Monument.

6 Padrão dos Descobrimentos (Discoveries Monument)

The monument, dedicated to Portugal's maritime quests and discovery of routes to the East, was built in 1960 by architect José Cotinelli Telmo and sculptor Leopoldo de Almeida, to mark the 500th anniversary of the death of Infante Henrique (Henry the Navigator).
Avenida de Brasília. Tel: 21 303 1950. You can cross the road to reach the Praça do Império.

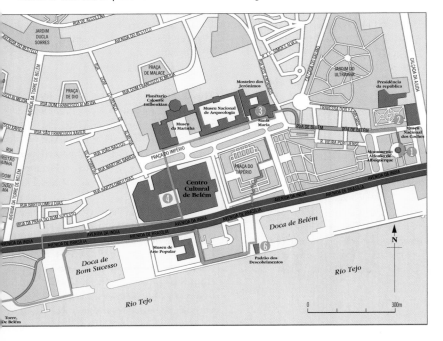

Centro Cultural de Belém (CCB) (Belém Cultural Centre)

Located in the historic district of Belém, the CCB is a private cultural centre that includes an Exhibition Centre, Performance Centre and Meeting Centre. Designed for the year that Portugal held its first presidency of the European Union, it has become a dynamic centre for cultural and leisure activities.

Entrance to the CCB's museums

The location of the modern cultural centre was chosen for two reasons. Firstly, this was the point of departure by the maritime navigators who set off in the hope of discovery. Secondly, it was here that the *Exposição do Mundo Português* (Exhibition of the Portuguese World) took place in the 1940s.

When the project was first decided upon in 1988, it was thrown out to international tender, with 57 designs submitted from around the world. In the end an Italian and Portuguese consortium was chosen. Architects Vittorio Gregotti and Manuel Salgado actually designed five sections of the centre, but only three were built – the Centro de Exposições (Exhibition Centre), Centro de Espectáculos (Performance Centre) and Centro de Reuniões (Meeting Centre),.

The Building

The project started in September 1988 and took five years to complete. The building is aesthetically unique, and the construction of the CCB proved somewhat of an engineering nightmare, requiring almost 3,000 concrete lintel supports.

Spread over 97,000m² (1,043,720 sq ft) and 6 hectares (15 acres), the different sections are connected by a pedestrian pathway running continuously both inside and out from the Praça do Império, as well as a series of bridges and ramps, with lakes, gardens and the Praça do Museu (Museum Square).

The CCB hosts exhibitions by internationally renowned artists

The CCB is a symbol of modernism and cultural life in Lisbon

The main entrance of the centre has a glass veranda and looks out on to the Praça do Império. Although the walls may seem austere, the CCB is a welcoming place where you can enjoy a drink or eat in the bar or restaurant while looking out over the river, or browse through the well stocked arts bookshop.

Centro de Exposições (Exhibition Centre)

This is probably the most interesting section for the visitor just passing through Belém. There are four galleries with numerous exhibition spaces plus the **Museu do Design** (Design Museum). The centre presents and produces exhibitions in fine art, architecture, design and photography by both up-and-coming and internationally renowned artists.

Centro de Espectáculos (Performance Centre)

This is the focal point of the CCB's artistic performances, including cinema, opera, ballet, theatre and various styles of music. It has a 1,400-seat Large Auditorium, a 300-seat Small Auditorium and an 85-seat space.

Centro de Reuniões (Meeting Centre)

This is a high-tech centre designed for meetings and congresses. It includes various shops, a restaurant, two bars and car parks and the CCB's administration centre.

Exhibition Centre; Praça do Império 1400; www.ccb.pt. Open: Tue–Sun 10am–7pm (last entrance 6.15pm). Other areas of the CCB open: daily 8.30am–9.45pm, until 2am when there are performances.

Gardens and Parks

Lisbon has a large number of beautiful green spaces tucked between its *bairros*. Whether they were the gardens of an old royal palace or are a newly claimed green space, they are a place to relax, to exercise and to cultivate both native and tropical flora. Gardens included in the walk on pages 44–45 are not repeated here.

Statue in Jardim Agricola Tropical

Jardim Agrícola Tropical
(Tropical Agricultural Garden)
Located in Belém, this garden was created with the aim of studying the flora in the old Portuguese colonies. Today it has a large collection of tropical plants including some palms from Madeira.
Calçada Galvão. Buses: 27, 28, 29, 43, 49, 51. Tram: 15. Open: Tue–Fri 10am–5pm, Sat & Sun 11am–6pm. Oct-May Sat & Sun 10am–5pm only.

Jardim Botánico da Ajuda
(Ajuda Botanical Garden)
Located by the Palácio Nacional da Ajuda, this is the oldest garden in Portugal – the Marquês de Pombal had it planted in 1768. It has been undergoing renovation, preserving its original botanical aims while presenting itself as a leisure space.
Calçada Ajuda. Open: July–Sept, 9am–8pm, Sept–July, 9am–6pm. Closed Wed, 25 Dec & 1 Jan. Admission charge. Tram: 18. Buses: 14, 27, 29, 32, 42, 60 & 73.

Jardim das Amoreiras
(Amoreiras Gardens)
The real name of these gardens is Marcelino Mesquita, named after the poet and writer of the same name. When inaugurated in 1759 by the Marquês de Pombal, there were 331 *amoreiras* (mulberry trees), with the objective of stimulating the Portuguese silk industry which was developing in a factory close to the square. The small garden has ten different species of tree, including some remaining mulberry trees. Look out for the collection of panels in Rúa das Amoreiras and the Mãe D'Agua.
Praça Amoreiras. Metro: Rato. Buses: 58 & 74.

Jardim do Campo Grande
(Campo Grande Gardens)
Set in a large area at the north end of the Avenida da República, this was a public park in the 16th century when it was known as Campo de Alvalade. In 1816, the first horse races took place here at the racing track built alongside. The gardens were remodelled in 1945, giving more recreational areas such as tennis courts, lakes, an ice rink, swimming pool and a shopping area. At the north end of the park there are statues of Dom Afonso Henriques and Dom João I, and a monument to the caricaturist Rafael Bordalo Pinheiro.

Campo Grande. Metro: Campo Grande.
Buses: 1, 3, 7, 17B, 21, 27, 31, 32, 35, 36,
38, 47, 55, 106 & 108.

Parque da Bela Vista
(Bela Vista Park)

Converted from an old farm in the east
of the city in 1991, the park has retained
its rural feel with large wooded areas.
Today a network of pathways give access

Statues in Parque Eduardo VII

to a picnic area and a *miradouro*
(belvedere), with a fantastic view over
the city and the River Tagus. There are
multi-sports and bathing areas, as well
as a golf course.
Avenida Dr. Arlindo Vicente. Metro: Bela
Vista. Buses: 5, 8, 10, 17, 19, 21, 22 & 55.

Parque Eduardo VII
(Edward VII Park)

Located at the north end of the Avenida
da Liberdade, this park marked a change
in the urban development of the city. It
was originally named after the avenue,
until King Edward VII of England
visited Lisbon in 1903. As well as
offering a great view over the city, there
is plenty to do here. On either side of its
large expanse of lawn and pathways,
there are exotic plants, areas for sports,
entertainment and eating. At the
northwestern end is the *Estufa Fria*,
where you can see all kinds of rare
plants.
Open: Apr–Sept, 9am–5.30pm, Oct–Mar,
9am–4.30pm. Admission charge.
Metro: Marquês de Pombal. Buses: 1, 2,
11, 12, 20, 22, 31, 101, 113 & 115.

Parque Florestal de Monsanto
(Monsanto Forest Park)

At almost 1,000 hectares (2,470 acres),
this is Lisbon's largest green space. Not
the kind of place you go for a stroll, it is
wise to go with a car and in company,
with something planned. The park has a
large campsite, mini-golf, tennis courts,
swimming pool, amphitheatre, shops
and restaurant, an exhibition centre and
outdoor activities for children.
Estrada Barcal, Monte das Perdizes.
Buses: 11, 14, 23, 24, 29, 43, 48 & 70.

Walk: São Pedro de Alcântara to Estrela

This walk takes in two of the city's best gardens, starting with a stroll from a great viewing point along a street full of antiques and ending by one of Lisbon's best-loved buildings, the Basílica da Estrela.

Allow 2–3 hours, but it really depends upon how long you linger in the parks. Start from Praça dos Restauradores. Take the Elevador da Glória next to the Palacio Foz, which comes every few minutes.

1 São Pedro de Alcântara

This is a pretty tree-lined *miradouro* (observation point) with great views over the Baixa and to the north of the city. At one end there is a fountain and also a statue dedicated to Eduardo Coelho (1855–89), founder of the national paper *Diario de Noticias*.
Walk right up Rúa Dom Pedro V, where you can window shop in the many antique and second-hand bookstores.

2 Praça do Príncipe Real

In a short while you come to the Príncipe Real Square, a large romantic green square with benches arranged in a circle under a large shady tree at one end and a café and children's play area at the other. Opened in 1860, today there is a museum located underneath it. The Museu da Agua (Water Museum) can be reached by steps at the centre of the square and is open most afternoons until 6pm.
Walk along the Rúa da Escola Politécnica and cross the road.

3 Jardim Botánico da Universidade de Lisboa (University of Lisbon Botanical Gardens)

The entrance to the Botanical Gardens is on the right-hand side, together with the Museu da Ciência. First planted in the 19th century, the gardens have a large number of rare tropical plants and the largest collection of *cicas* (tall palms) in the country, as well as plants from the age of the dinosaurs, collections of palms, cacti and fleshy plants.

Take a relaxing stroll amongst lakes, bridges and statues. The small admission charge is worth this sanctuary in the city.
Calçada da Ajuda. Tel: 21 362 2503.
Open: 9am–6pm. Closed Wed.
Come back on to the Rúa da Escola Politécnica and cross the road to Rúa da Imprensa Nacional, a residential street with a hodgepodge of different architectural styles. At the end of this steep stroll downwards, take a left and first right on to Rúa de Santo Amaro. This is a steep climb upwards.

The Jardim Botânico is filled with tropical plants

4 Jardim da Estrela

At the top of the road you can relax in the Jardim da Estrela, with its benches and café, toddler's play park, bandstand and swans on the lake. The garden is also called Jardim Guerra Junqueiro and was laid out in the mid-19th century.
Walk across the park, bearing left past the

café. Across the road you will see the Basílica da Estrela.

5 Basílica da Estrela

This large building, with its white dome, is one of Lisbon's great landmarks. Built on orders of Dona Maria I (1779–89), it displays evidence of the design by the Mafra school of architects. Inside, the faded walls are decorated with Portuguese marble and paintings by Italian masters.
Largo da Estrela. Tel: 21 396 0915.
Walk around the park along Rua de S Bernardo and on to Avda Pedro Alvares Cabral to get to the Rato metro station. Alternatively you can take Tram No 28 to the Chiado and beyond from outside the Basilica.

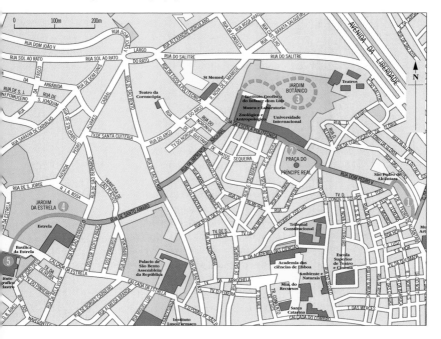

Fundação Calouste Gulbenkian

The Calouste Gulbenkian Foundation is Portugal's most important cultural organisation, boasting the country's most renowned orchestra and ballet, in addition to museums, exhibition spaces, an auditorium, arts library and lush gardens. It also aims to promote education, production and research in the areas of both science and the arts. Designed by architects Ruy Athouguia, Pedro Cid and Alberto Pessoa, the headquarters are located in the heart of Lisbon in the Gulbenkian Park, designed by Ribeiro Telles.

Av de Berna, 45A.

Oriental ornament inside the Museo Gulbenkian

Ballet Gulbenkian

Founded in 1965, the ballet has evolved with each artistic director incorporating the new trends and styles of the time while retaining the classical repertoire. It promotes the careers of national dancers and choreographers, and so the company mainly consists of Portuguese dancers. Today's artistic director, Iracity Cardoso, continues to develop the ballet in the same way.

Coro Gulbenkian

Formed in 1964, the Gulbenkian Choir is now 100 strong. This does not restrict it though; it sings

Enjoy the garden sculptures

the 1950s. As well as works by the most representative 20th-century Portuguese artists, there are some Modernist works from overseas, a special British art section from the late 1950s and various works by Armenian artists.
Tel: 21 782 3000.

Museu Gulbenkian
The Gulbenkian Museum houses an eclectic collection, mostly brought together by its founder. Divided into various permanent galleries, the pieces are organised according to chronology and geography. The first section of the museum moves through Egyptian, Greco-Roman, Mesopotamian, Eastern Islamic, Armenian and Far Eastern art. The second covers European art with sections dedicated to sculpture, painting, decorative art and the art of the book, covering a diverse cross-section of the most representative artists from the 11th to the mid-20th centuries.
Tel: 21 782 3461.

a cappella with just a handful of the choir members performing 16th and 17th-century Portuguese pieces, and collaborates with the Gulbenkian Orchestra to put on Classical or Romantic choral symphonies and performs both Portuguese and international contemporary works. Michel Corboz has been its choral director since 1969 and is assisted by Fernando Eldoro and Jorge Matta.

Museu de Arte Moderna
Founded in 1983, the museum contains work collected by the foundation since

Orquestra Gulbenkian
Founded in 1962, the Gulbenkian Orchestra is the most important orchestral group in Portugal. Apart from its domestic programme, the orchestra has also toured most of Europe and parts of Africa. For more than 30 years, many of the most respected soloists and conductors have been included in the orchestra's programmes, but it is particularly well known for its recordings under the direction of Michel Corboz. Lawrence Foster took over as music director in the 2002–3 season.

Fado is the most renowned form of Portuguese folk music, and one that draws in thousands of tourists to the fado houses of the Bairro Alto and the Alfama in Lisbon. Promoted for years as a sanitised, colourful form of national music by the Salazar dictatorship, fado has now been revealed in its bare form, reflecting the *saudade* (or nostalgic yearning) of its origins and the destiny of its meaning.

Fado is sung by a solo vocalist, traditionally accompanied by a *viola* (Spanish guitar) and a *guitarra* (pear-shaped, 12-string Portuguese guitar).

In fact, there are two main forms of fado: from Lisbon and Coimbra. Both have distinct origins and performance styles. Fado from Coimbra developed amongst upper-class students of the University of Coimbra, who traditionally perform a lighter, more lyrical form of the genre, dressed in the black capes of the university with the instruments tuned slightly differently from the Lisbon style.

While both forms are reputed to have developed from troubadour songs, Lisbon's fado developed amongst the lower classes as a disreputable form of music. Sung by social outcasts and rowdy sailors, much of the melancholy and *saudade* of this form comes from expressions of lost loves and livelihoods. It was also closely linked to the Discoveries, with sailors singing of their yearning for their homeland, the *fado do marinheiro*.

Although it is thought that the development of fado dates back centuries, the first mention of the genre can only be traced to around 1840, and some believe it was influenced by Brazilian *modinha* and *lundum*. Around this time fado saw its first *superstar*, Maria Severa, from the old Lisbon neighbourhood of Mouraria. A song of suffering and the fight against power, during the 19th century fado became popularised and, over time, respected by the upper classes.

Today fado is still performed in the older areas of Lisbon, in the *vadio fado* houses of the Bairro Alto and Alfama, where you eat, drink and listen to the spontaneous performances by amateur singers. People shout approval and sometimes join in. However, there are also professional fado houses, where you can have a meal and listen to four or five singers until the early hours of the morning. Some stars of fado even perform in concert halls.

The recording industry widened the popularity of fado, with people like Amália Rodrigues and Carlos do Carmo becoming internationally renowned, but still performing in small cafés. Other famous fado singers have included Alfredo Marceneiro, Maria Teresa do Noronha, Antonio Pinto Basto and Nuno Da Camara Pereira. The 1990s saw the success of Madredeus, with the beautiful voice of Maria Teresa Salgueiro accompanied by the haunting sounds of accordion, guitars, bass and cello.

AMÁLIA RODRIGUES

The spread of fado's renown around the world owes much to the recordings of Amália Rodrigues. The daughter of a poor amateur Lisbon musician, Rodrigues started her career singing in cafés, but rose to fame in the 1950s and 1960s with recordings of songs such as 'Uma Casa Portuguesa'.

Considered as the premier *fadista*, when Rodrigues died in October 1999 she was given a funeral worthy of a head of state. She also became the first woman to be entombed in the Panteão Nacional (National Pantheon) in Lisbon, alongside kings and queens and other important figures in the history of Portugal. Furthermore, at the top of Lisbon's Parque Eduardo VII, the Jardim Amália was named after the singer.

Facing page: Fado performances can be emotional
Left: The beautiful and legendary Amália Rodrigues

Alfama

Typical Alfama Street

Originally of Arab origins, the ancient district of Alfama was the first fortified area of Lisbon and home to the wealthier people of Lisbon. Over time, the royal family and the rich moved out and it became a poor neighbourhood. Although it survived the Great Earthquake, today the buildings are dilapidated and run down, patched up by the locals, reflecting the poverty that much of its population has lived in for the last few hundred years.

The community is tight, however, with its own network of communication, a grapevine that moves from mouth to mouth through the windows, across the narrow streets and lines of washing, down the steps towards the river.

Casa dos Bicos

Brás de Albuquerque, son of Alfonso de Albuquerque, the Viceroy of India, built the Casa dos Bicos from 1523–30, close to the shipyards and customs houses along the riverfront, in a time of prosperity for Lisbon. Called the 'House of the Peaks', the building's facade is covered in pyramid-like peaks with a quadrangular base. Today, little of the original building remains, having suffered especially in the Great Earthquake of 1755. It became a warehouse for many years, until declared a National Monument in 1910. Bought by the Portuguese authorities in 1963, it has undergone a process of reconstruction to form a museum inside which hosts temporary exhibitions.
Rua dos Bacalhoeiros. Tel: 21 888 4827. Buses: 1, 13, 46 & 91.

Castelo de São Jorge

The Castelo de São Jorge is the crown on top of the hill. Originally built by the Moors in the 8th century, they were driven out by Dom Afonso Henriques in 1147. Spread over an area of 6,000m (19,690ft), the castle grounds are surrounded by a dry moat. Inside there are various towers, lookouts (or viewing points today) and two squares.

Southeast of the battlements you can still see the cobbled streets of Santa Cruz, an old neighbourhood with a medieval church containing a 17th-century statue of St George.
Tel: 21 887 7244.

Feira da Ladra

Commonly known as the 'thieves market', this is a mishmash of bargains and junk. If you like flea markets, this is the place to come for a rummage.
Campo de Sta Clara. Open: 7.30am–1pm Tue & Sat.

Igreja de Santa Engrácia

This church is the National Pantheon – a striking building started in 1682 and

finished in 1966. There are cenotaphs of important figures in Portuguese history – Vasco da Gama, Afonso de Albuquerque, Henry the Navigator, Luis Vaz de Camões. Take the lift for a panorama of the city.
Campo de Santa Clara. Tel: 21 888 1520. Open: Tue–Sun 10am–5pm.

Igreja de São Vicente de Fora
The church was founded in the 12th century by Dom Afonso Henriques, to thank the saint for his successful conquest of Lisbon. Look out for the Baroque nave with its forged iron trelliswork and the choir floor with wood from Brazil.
Largo de São Vicente. Tel: 21 882 4400. Open: Tue–Fri 9am–6pm, Sat 9am–7pm, Sun 9am–12.30am & 3–5pm. Tram: 28. Bus: 12.

Jewish quarter
The old Jewish quarter today is a poor area with narrow streets and archways, home to a variety of people including those from Mozambique and Cape Verde Islands (*see p53*).

Miradouro de Santa Luzia
This belvedere offers a panoramic view of the Alfama and the River Tagus, with

The battlements of the Castelo de São Jorge

the National Pantheon and the Mosteiro de São Vicente da Fora to the left and the Igreja de São Miguel below. Along one side there are *azulejos* panels showing views of Lisbon before the Great Earthquake and the Christians attacking the Castelo de São Jorge.
Rua do Limoeiro. Tram: 28.

Museu das Artes Decorativas
Decorated in the style of an 18th-century aristocratic residence, the museum contains important Portuguese *azulejos* and furniture and textiles (*see p29*).
Largo das Portas do Sol, 2. Open: Tue–Sun 10am–5pm. Admission charge. Trams: 12 & 28. Bus: 37.

Museu Militar
The museum has a large display of artillery, war relics and paintings dating back to the 15th century (*see p30*).
Largo do Museu da Artilharia. Open: Tue–Sun 10am–5pm. Closed public holidays. Buses: 9, 12, 25, 28, 35, 39, 46, 104, 105 & 107.

Sé Catedral
Built by Dom Afonso Henriques, Portugal's first king, in the 12th century, the cathedral is a mixture of Gothic and Romanesque architectural styles. Although it retains parts of its original structure, the cathedral suffered badly during the Great Earthquake of 1755. It was renovated and today houses a small museum.
Largo da Sé. Tel: 21 886 6752. Cathedral open: Sun–Mon 9am–5pm, Tue–Sat 9am–7pm; Museum & Treasury open: 10am–1pm & 2–5pm. Tram 28. Bus 37.

Walk: Alfama

This walk takes you from the Castelo de São Jorge at the top of the hill back down to the River Tagus; descending from the fantastic view over the city through the heart of this historic residential district, past the Sé Cathedral and the Casa dos Bicos.

Start by taking Tram No 28 to Largo das Portas do Sol in the Alfama (you'll know it because many other tourists get off here and also because of the view).

Allow 2–3 hours.

1 Largo das Portos do Sol
This viewing point enjoys great vistas over the Alfama and a café if you want to start out with some refreshment.
Walk across the road.

2 Museu das Artes Decorativas
Here you will see the Museu das Artes Decorativas (*see p29*) with its collection of Portuguese *azulejos*, furniture and textiles.

Passing Sé Catedral in Tram 28

Walk up the street on the left-hand side of the museum and take the first right, Travessa de Santa Luzia. At the top by the A Tasquinha restaurant, there is a sign to the right for the Castelo. Go up here and you come to the castle wall. Follow it round to the left, through the archway.

3 Castelo de São Jorge (St George's Castle)
On the left-hand side you will see a glassed-in statue of São Jorge, the Protector of Portugal and the castle's namesake. As you continue round to the right you see the Casa do Governador, today a book and gift shop. Through the gate on the left you come to the Praça de Armas, with a statue of Afonso Henriques on the left and a viewing area over Lisbon and the River Tagus. As you walk around the wall, you come to an *azulejos* panel pointing out places in the city. There is also the exclusive restaurant, Casa do Leão, on the right. Just past here turn right and you will find your way through to the battlements, which you can explore.

Come out of the battlements and continue straight ahead past the café to return to the castle gate.

Retrace your steps towards the Largo das Portas do Sol, turning right at the end of Largo do Contador Mor.

4 Miradouro de Santa Luzia

You will come out on to the Miradouro de Santa Luzia, with the church of the same name to the left. There are fantastic views from here and on the right-hand side you will see *azulejos* depicting ancient Lisbon.

Walk round the Igreja de Santa Luzia and down the steps on the other side, Rua Norberto de Araújo. On the right-hand side you can see the remnants of Moorish walls. Continue until you see the steps on the left. Go down here (Beco da Corvinha) to Largo de Cantina. Walk straight across to Largo de São Miguel at the front of São Miguel Church. This route takes you through the heart of the Alfama and its winding alleyways. From here turn right down Rua São Miguel. Now you have two options before proceeding onto Casa dos Bicos.

5 Jewish quarter

If you turn left after the shops, you will wind down through the very poor and narrow streets that used to be the Jewish quarter. It ends with an archway that opens on to the Rua Cais Santarém.

Turn right and walk down to the Casa dos Bicos or retrace your steps back up to the shops. Continue straight ahead at the shops (or turn left if you have come back from the Jewish Quarter) along João da Praça. Bear left past the church and continue for another block.

6 Sé Catedral

On the right-hand side you will see Sé Catedral, with its variety of architectural styles, Gothic cloisters and treasury with a collection of silver and religious relics.

Walk back down the street and turn right to get down to the main road. Turn right here and walk down to the most distinctive building on the right.

7 Casa dos Bicos

You will find the building around 100m (328ft) along the street, situated next to two restaurants. You can sit here and have some refreshment while looking at the building or go inside if there is a temporary exhibition.

To get back to the Baixa continue straight along this street.

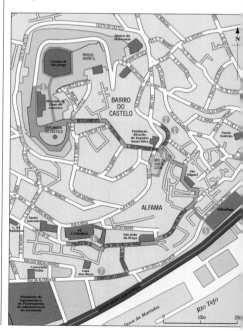

Lisbon's most famous and devastating earthquake struck on 1 November 1755 at 9.30am, ripping up the remaining beautiful Moorish buildings and bringing the city forward from its medieval past and dragging it into the Enlightenment. Centred in the Atlantic, three tremors over a ten-minute period were felt in North Africa and as far as Italy and, although damage was widespread, Lisbon was the largest and most important city to suffer.

The fire that followed the earthquake caused the most damage, and was started by abandoned cooking fires when people fled their homes, and candles burning in churches. Exacerbated by looters ransacking the houses, the fires raged out of control for five days, cutting off squares and narrow streets. The fire destroyed an area from the Carmo Convent to Rossio Square, burning down palaces, churches and houses. It moved towards the

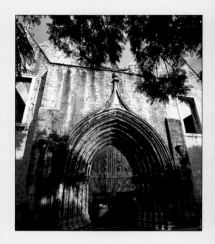

Castelo de São Jorge but, thankfully, the Bairro Alto and Alfama districts were only partially burned.

As if the earthquake was not enough, about 30 minutes later a strong tsunami (tidal wave) hit, ravaging the coasts of Portugal, Southern Spain and Morocco. Those that had taken refuge in the water during the earthquake were dragged out to sea by waves of up to 6m (19.5ft) high. The western part of the city around Alcântara suffered most, but the tsunami also reached the Terreiro do Paço (Praça do Comércio). The city's population of 250,000 was diminished by at least 15,000, with further devastation in other parts of the country.

Emerging out of the smoke, Lisbon was faced with the logistical problem of rebuilding a large section of the city. Churches and other buildings had

suffered irreparable damage, and there was rubble everywhere. With buildings higher than the width of the streets they fell into, rescue attempts and the clear-up process were hindered.

During this time, when scientific, rational thought was emerging, the spiritual world came into question. Of course, there was more scepticism and division between the church's explanation of the disaster and the scientific explanations of natural phenomena. As first-hand accounts leaked beyond the borders of Portugal, the world's attention turned to the Portuguese capital. The Great Earthquake became the first natural disaster of the modern world, with numerous depictions produced in art and literature, as well as essays by philosophers such as Voltaire.

The city was rebuilt by the Marquês de Pombal. He curbed both travel by boat and movement through the city to control removal of vital resources and labour power, and set about reconstructing the city. The area between the Terreiro do Paço and the Praça de Rossio, which previously had a mixture of winding narrow streets and luxurious palaces, was rebuilt with neo-classical buildings with uniform facades on a grid-like structure. This attracted a mercantile class and 'enlightened' notions of equality. Nobility could still live there, but with the outward appearance of everyone else.

The Terreiro do Paço, where the Royal Palace had previously stood, became known as the Praça do Comércio, with the streets that led northwards named after the mercantile functions of those that lived and worked there. The streets that ran across these were named after the church, and the other streets after the monarchy. However, a statue of the monarch, João I (who ruled from 1750–77), was built at the centre of the Praça do Comércio.

Facing page below: *Azulejos* panel in Igreja de Santa Lucia, depicting pre-earthquake Lisbon
Facing page above: Igreja do Carmo
Above: King José I's statue dominates the Praça do Comércio

The Baixa

The Baixa is one of the city's focal points, lying between the Praça do Comércio and Avenida da Liberdade. Rebuilt under the direction of the Marquês de Pombal, following the destruction of the city in the Great Earthquake of 1755, the Baixa is structured on a grid system. Although not all the buildings remain from the Pombaline era, the structure of the neighbourhood has stayed. The area buzzes with life during the day, as tourists and shoppers wander around the streets, but at night it becomes deserted.

From the top of the Elevador Santa Justa you can see over the Baixa

The Praça do Comércio lies at the river entrance to the Baixa. This recently renovated square is often still called the Terreiro de Paço after the Paços da Ribeira royal palace that stood here before the 1755 Great Earthquake. Today a bronze statue of Dom José I, king at that time, dominates the square, which has led to the nickname of Black Horse Square. Designed by Joaquim Machado de Castro, the statue is actually more green than black now.

This is also one of the places in the Baixa where typical Pombaline structures remain – functional and unfussy. It houses a mixture of ministries, cafés, shops and the Lisbon Welcome Centre. In the northeast corner, the most famous of these cafés is the Martinho da Arcada which, along with the Café A Brasileira in the Bairro Alto, was a place where artists and writers would meet. On the north side of the square stands the Arco Triunfal, designed by Veríssimo José da Costa in 1755 and finally finished in 1873. The arch is topped with images of glory and

valour, and contains famous figures such as Pombal and Vasco da Gama. It is also the entrance way to Rua Augusta, the focal point of the Baixa streets and the main pedestrian route, with numerous market stalls along the way.

Many of the names of the streets in the grid reflect the trades of the people that once lived and worked there. Rua do Ouro was where goldsmiths worked, Rua da Prata, the silversmiths and Rua dos Sapateiros, the shoemakers. There are still numerous jewellery shops throughout the Baixa, along with shoe shops, bookshops, lace shops, stationers and tobacconists. International boutiques have appeared in the past few years.

At the junction of Rua do Ouro and Rua Santa Justa is one of the Baixa's most prominent structures, the Elevador Santa Justa. Built at the beginning of the 20th century by French architect Raoul Mesnier du Ponsard, this iron structure links the Baixa and the Bairro Alto. However, due to structural problems, access is suspended. A restaurant and café at the top of the lift are still open and offer great views over the Baixa.

At the north end of the grid are two squares, the Praça da Figueira and the larger Praça Dom Pedro IV (Rossio). In the latter stands a statue of Dom Pedro IV, who gave independence to Brazil and was a hero of Portuguese liberalism.

At the north end of the square is the Teatro Nacional D Maria II. Built in the 1840s by Italian architect Fortunato Lodi in the neo-classical style popular at that time, the theatre was virtually destroyed by fire but rebuilt once again by Rebello de Andrade. To the left of the theatre is Rossio Station, which was built by José Luis Monteiro from 1886–7. The building displays *Neomanuelino* characteristics (*see p33*) and the façade has two prominent horseshoe archways.

Beyond here are the Praça dos Restauradores and Avenida da Liberdade. The square was named after the War of Restoration, which won back Portugal's independence from Spain in 1640, and at the centre is a monument of commemoration to those who fought.

The Avenida da Liberdade was built on top of the Pombaline Passeio Público in 1879, with the Praça dos Restauradores at the south end and a monument to the Marquês de Pombal at the north. It was built in the modern boulevard style, with trees and kiosks along its length, and in the years after its construction, grand residential buildings and the Tivoli theatre, amongst others, sprung up. Today the avenue remains at the heart of the city.

Images of glory and valour top the Arco Triunfal in the Praça do Comércio

Walk: Baixa

This walk starts at the most famous square in Lisbon, the Praça do Comércio, and continues through the Arco Triunfal into the heart of the Baixa. It ends at the Elevador Santa Justa.

Start in the Praça do Comércio.

1 Praça do Comércio
Walk through the centre of what is often referred to as Black Horse Square to see the bronze statue of Dom José I. From the centre you also get the full impact of the Pombaline architecture and archways. On the north side you will see the tremendous Arco Triunfal.
Walk through the archway to Rua Augusta.

2 Rua Augusta
The main paved walkway through the Baixa grid, this street is full of fashion shops, cafés and street performers.
Continue along this street and zigzag as you like to Rua da Prata, two streets to the right.

3 Praça Dom Pedro IV (Rossio)
You come out on to Praça da Figueira, a plain Pombaline square lined with shops and cafés with a statue of Dom João I at the centre. If you walk to the left you come to the Praça Dom Pedro IV, commonly known as Rossio.
Walk to the left of the theatre.

4 Praça dos Restauradores
This large square is dedicated to those who fought in the War of Restoration, and there is a monument to the war in the centre. On the far side you will see the former Palácio Foz. Today it houses the Ministry of Culture.

5 Estação do Rossio (Rossio Station)
Opposite you will see Rossio Station with its two *Neomanuelino* horseshoe archways.
Continue along the road and take the first right and left on to Rua das Portas de Santo Antão. Just after this theatre, turn left back on to the Praça dos Restauradores. From here you can either take a stroll up the Avenida da Liberdade, or retrace your steps back to the Baixa grid going down Rua do Ouro on the right.

6 Elevador Santa Justa
The elevator is located on Rua de Santa Justa on the right. Designed by Raul Ponsard and opened in 1902, it was originally called the Elevador do Carmo and is a good example of post-Eiffel ironwork.

You can enjoy a great view of the Baixa from the café and restaurant at the top.
Open Mon–Sat 7am–11pm; Sun & public holidays 9am–11pm.
From here you can continue on to the Chiado and Bairro Alto Walk (pp60–1) or walk round to the Baixa-Chiado metro station just off Rúa do Carmo.

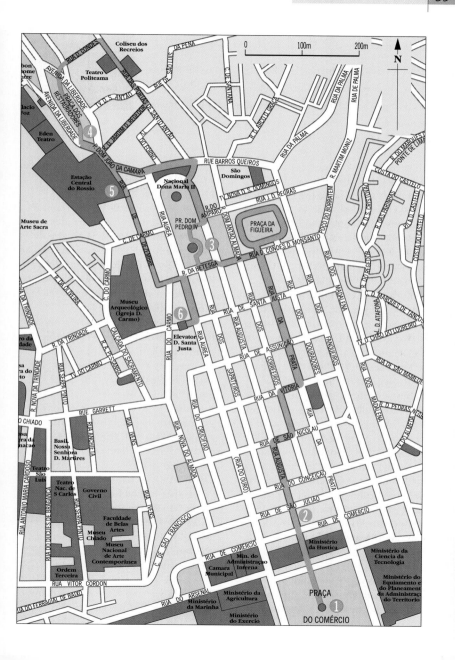

Chiado and Bairro Alto

Renowned for its literary and artistic connections, this is the liveliest area in Lisbon with plenty of bars and restaurants. Set on top of a hill and overlooking the Baixa, the area leads down towards the River Tagus.

A Chiado street

You can get here in various ways. From the Baixa, you can walk up, but if your legs aren't up to it take the **Elevador da Glória** from Restauradores. This takes you up to the fabulous *miradouro* of **São Pedro de Alcântara**, which offers superb views over the city. You used to be able to take the Santa Justa elevator up to the Largo do Carmo but today you can only go to the viewing tower at the top. However, if you don't fancy the lift or walking, take the metro to Baixa-Chiado or Tram 28 from the Baixa, which also runs onto Estrela.

There is a little of everything here and a large dose of fun. From the fashionable shops of the Chiado, renovated following a disastrous fire, to the antique shops and second-hand bookshops all along **Rua D Pedro V**, shopping can be done at a leisurely pace. There are plenty of places to take refreshment but top of the list are the **Solar do Vinho do Porto** (*see p66*) and the **Café A Brasileira.**

Open since 1905, Café A Brasileira was once frequented by Lisbon's favourite modern poet, Fernando Pessoa (*see pp62–3*) and his contemporaries – it is still the gathering point for writers and artists today. Stop for *uma bica* (a coffee) and admire the gilded mirror interior of the café or sit outside beside

the bronze statue of Pessoa. There is also a restaurant downstairs. *Rua Garrett, 120. Tel: 21 346 9541. Open: daily 8–2am. Metro: Baixa-Chiado. Tram: 28.*

If it's a relaxing time you're after from the **Miradouro de São Pedro de Alcântara** you can head past the antique shops to the **Praça do Principe Real**, a green and romantic square with plenty of seating, and then move on to the **Jardim Botânico** (*see pp44–5*).

The crown of the Bairro Alto, though, is the **Igreja do Carmo.** This Gothic church was completed in 1423 and destroyed by the 1755 earthquake that devastated much of the city. Today its ruins tower over the city as a monument to the disaster. Alongside is an archaeological museum (**Museu Arqueológico do Carmo**) with relics from pre-history to the early modern period. *Largo Carmo. Tel: 21 346 0473. Open: Mon–Sat 10am–1pm & 2–5pm.*

Another worthwhile visit is the **Igreja São Roque** and **Museu de Arte Sacra.** This Jesuit church was built in the 16th century and expanded in the 18th century with the building of the Capela de São João, designed by Italian architects Luigi Vanvitelli and Nicola Salvi. Next to the church there is the Museu de Arte Sacra. Other museums include the **Museu do Chiado** and the **Museu Nacional de Arte Contemporânea** (*see pp74-75*).

Whilst you're here, you can hop on to tram 28 towards Estrela. As well as the Basilica (*see pp44–5*) you can see the **Palácio de São Bento**.

Construction started on the building in 1598 and by 1615 it had become home to Benedictine monks. The monastery was dissolved in the 19th century and in 1834 the building became the seat of the *Assambleia da República* (parliament). Unfortunately you can only look from the outside, unless you get a special appointment or you go to watch parliament in session (*Wednesday or Thursday from 3pm or Friday from 10am*). *Rua de São Bento.*

To end the day on a cultural note you can see a performance at the **Teatro Nacional de São Carlos.** Built from 1792–5 by José da Costa, it replaced the old opera house that stood here before the earthquake. Alternatively eat, drink and listen to some typical music in one of the many **fado houses** (*see pp146–53*).

Relax with good company outside the Brasileira Café

The most celebrated Portuguese poet, Fernando Pessoa, was one of the most original poets of European modernism and at the forefront of its development in Portugal. Born in Lisbon in 1888, Pessoa's father died of tuberculosis when he was five years old. His mother's remarriage a year later, to the Portuguese consul in South Africa, led to their relocation there.

In Durban, Pessoa learned English, and the influence of his time there is reflected in the fact that his first three books of poetry were in English (*Antinous*, 1918; *Sonnets*, 1918; and *English Poems*, 1921). His first book in

Portuguese (*Mensagem*) only appeared in 1934. However, Lisbon was very much part of his soul and he returned to the city at the age of 17, studying briefly at the University of Lisbon from 1906.

After dropping out of university, Pessoa made his money from translating and writing business letters in English and French. He started his literary career in 1912, beginning with literary criticism and moving on to creative prose and poetry. He believed that literary texts should be appreciated for themselves and not because of the association with the author's name. This begins to explain why he wrote under numerous pseudonyms and heteronyms.

While Pessoa asserted that under a pseudonym he wrote as himself, with his heteronymic work he wrote through an alter ego, writing outside himself. Each of his heteronyms, from Alberto Caeiro and Ricardo Reis to Alvaro de Campos and the semi-heteronym Bernardo Soares, had a biography and physical attributes as well as politics and religion.

Much of Pessoa's work was published in literary journals and magazines. Although he did frequent the Café A Brasileria (in the Bairro Alto, *see p60*) and the Martinho (in the Baixa), where he read and wrote and occasionally met people, he generally kept a low profile. Much of his work was not read (or published) until after his death, yet Paul Buck asserts in his book, *Lisbon* (2002),

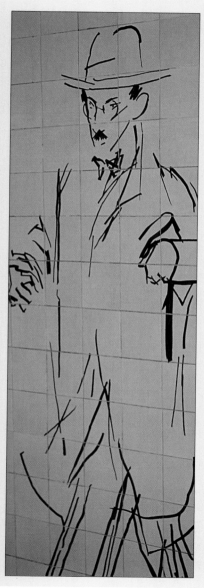

that Lisbon is very much Pessoa's city and he left his stamp on the city in numerous ways. Lisbon is at the heart of much of Pessoa's work, from his major prose work, *The Book of Disquietude* (1982) by Bernardo Soares, to *Lisbon: What the Tourist Should See* (1992). Other works include *Poesias de Alvaro de Campos* (1944), *Odes to Ricardo Reis* (1946), *Cartas de Amor* (1978) and *Always Astonished: Selected Prose* (1988).

Pessoa died in November 1935 from cirrhosis of the liver, leaving a trunk with more than 25,000 pieces of poetry, letters and journals by a variety of his heteronyms. Today he is widely acclaimed and treasured in Lisbon, where a bronze statue permanently sits at a table outside A Brasileira.

To learn more about the author, you can visit the Casa Fernando Pessoa, where he lived. Created in honour of the poet, this is also a place where poetry recitals take place. As well as tours, there is a library within the building.

Rua Coelho da Rocha, 16–18. Tel: 21 396 8190; www.casafernandopessoa.com/. Open: Mon–Fri 10am–6pm (except Thur 1–8pm). Buses: 9, 20 & 38. Trams: 25 & 38. Metro: Rato.

Facing page: Pessoa still sits in contemplation outside the Brasileira
This page: Pessoa waits for the metro at Alto dos Moinhos station

Walk: Chiado and Bairro Alto

This walk starts at the historic ruins of the Carmo Convent and ends at the Solar do Vinho do Porto.
Allow 2–3 hours

Start at the Largo do Carmo. Unless the Elevador de Santa Justa is renovated to

Praça Luis de Camões with a statue of the author at the centre

allow access from the Baixa to the Bairro Alto, you will have to walk up the Calçada da Glória, or take the metro to Baixa-Chiado and walk up, or take the easier option of riding the Elevador da Glória from Restauradores and walking down.

1 Igreja do Carmo

Behind the east side of Largo do Carmo lie the ruins of the Carmo Church, a Gothic Carmelite Church destroyed in the Great Earthquake of 1755, just months after completion. You can visit the Museu de Arqueologia, with findings from the Visigoths and the Romans as well as pieces found in the Americas.
Tel: 21 346 0473.
Walk across the square to Travessa do Carmo and on the left you will see a sign for Rúa Garrett that takes you through some new buildings. These were designed by Alvaro Siza, the country's leading architect (see pp74–5), to reconstruct the area of Chiado destroyed by fire in 1988. Go down the escalator on to the street.

2 Rúa Garrett

You will find yourself on Rúa Garrett, named after the Porto-born writer (*see p97*).
Go right, up the street.

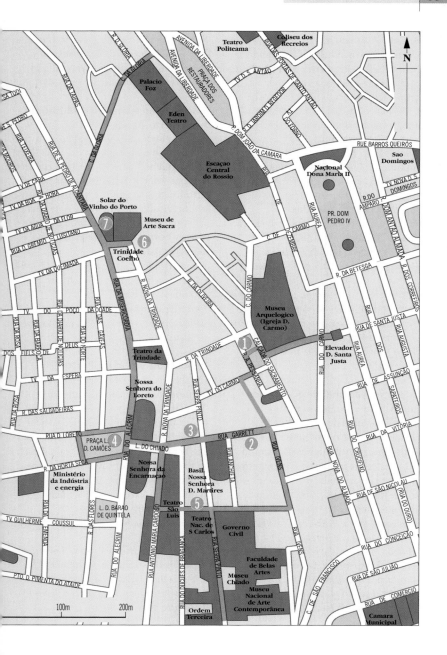

Teatro Politeama

Coliseu dos Recreios

AVENIDA DA LIBERDADE

PRAÇA DOS RESTAURADORES

AVENIDA DA LIBERDADE

TV. DA GLORIA

R. DAS PORTAS DE SANTO ANTÃO

TV. D. S. ANTÃO

Palacio Foz

Eden Teatro

C. DA GLORIA

R. DOM JOÃO DA CAMARA

R. DO JARDIM DO REGEDOR

AL.

COFEDRO

RUE BARROS QUEIRÓS

Sao Domingos

Escaçao Central do Rossio

Nacional Dona Maria II

TV. NOVA D. S. DOMINGOS

R. DO AMPARO

DOM ANTÃO ALMADA

R. DOS CORREEIROS

Solar do Vinho do Porto

Museu de Arte Sacra

⑦

⑥

Trinidade Coelho

PR. DOM PEDRO IV

C. DE SETEMBRO

RUA AUREA

R. DA BETESGA

RUA DE SANTA JUSTA

RUA AUGUSTA

Museu Arquelogico (Igreja D. Carmo)

C. DO CARMO

Elevador D. Santa Justa

RUA AUREA

RUA DAS

Teatro da Trindade

R. DA TRINDADE

①

CALÇADA DO SACRAMENTO

R. DA ASSUNÇÃO

Nossa Senhora do Loreto

R. NOVA DA TRINDADE

R. DA OLIVEIRA

R. DO CARMO

R. DA VITÓRIA

RUA DO CRUCIFIXO

RUA NOVA DO ALMADA

③

RUA GARRETT

②

RUA IVENS

RUA ANCHIETA

PRAÇA L. D. CAMÕES

④

L. DO CHIADO

RUA D. LORETO

RUA DO ALECRIM

Nossa Senhora da Encarnação

Basil. Nossa Senhora D. Martires

Ministério da Indústria e energia

R. DA HORTA SECA

RAS FLORES

L. D. BARÃO DE QUINTELA

Teatro São Luis

⑤

RUA ANTONIO MARIA CARDOSO

RUA SERPA PINTO

RUA NOVA DO ALMADA

RUA DE SÃO NICOLAU (RUA DO OURO)

TV. GUILHERME COUSSUL

Teatro Nac. de S Carlos

Governo Civil

RUA DO ALECRIM

PTO. D. PIMENTA DO ATAIDE

RUA DUQUES DE BRAGANÇA

Faculdade de Belas Artes

Museu Chiado

Museu Nacional de Arte Contemporânea

RUA DE SÃO NICOLAU

RUA DO CONCEIÇÃO

C. DE SÃO FRANCISCO

RUA DE SÃO JULIÃO

Ordem Terceira

Camara Municipal

RUA DE COMERCIO

100m   200m

N

3 Café A Brasileira

On the right-hand side is the literary haunt, Café A Brasileira, where Lisbon poet Fernando Pessoa and other renowned writers used to meet. The first table at the top of the stairs is still the gathering point for writers and artists every morning.
Rúa Garrett, 120. Tel: 21 346 9541.
Just after the café, you will come to the Praça Luis de Camões.

4 Praça Luis de Camões

At the centre of the square you will see a statue of another of Lisbon's most famous writers, Luis de Camões.
Retrace your steps back past the two churches that stand on either side of Rúa Garrett and turn right on to Rúa António Maria Cardoso. On the left you will see the Teatro São Luis and just before there is a small street, the Travessa Teatros, go down here and down the steps at the other end.

5 Teatro Nacional de São Carlos

You will find yourself in front of the Teatro Nacional de São Carlos that replaced the old opera house in the late 18th century. Although visits around the theatre are not generally permitted, there are occasionally exhibitions next to the foyer, allowing you to glimpse its Rococo interior.
Rúa Serpa Pinto, 9. Tel: 21 325 3045. Turn right down Rua de Serpa Pinto for the Museu Chiado or the Museu Nacional de Arte Contemporânea. Otherwise, retrace your steps towards the Praça Luis de Camões. Just after the two churches of Nossa Senhora do Loreta and Nossa Senhora da Encarnaçao that straddle Rúa Garrett, turn right on to Rúa da Miseracórdia. This steep street will lead you up to the Trindade Coelho square.

6 Igreja São Roque and Museu de Arte Sacra

On the north side of the square you will see a church and museum. The Igreja São Roque was built in the 16th century and has some *azulejos* from this period. Also worth seeing is the *trompe l'oeil* ceiling. Inside the Museu de Arte Sacra you can learn more about the church's history as well view its selection of sacred art and relics.
Largo Trinidade Coelho. Tel: 21 323 5381. Open: Tue–Sun 10am–5pm. Buses: 58, 100; metro: Baixa–Chiado.
Continue along the street you were on, which now becomes the Rúa de São Pedro de Alcântara.

7 Solar do Vinho do Porto

On the left, at No 45, you will see the entrance to the Solar do Vinho do Porto. This is a great opportunity to find out about the Portuguese fortified wine if you don't have time to visit Porto, and the perfect place to end the walk. Relax in the armchairs of this 18th-century mansion, while sampling some of the hundreds of varieties of Port held behind the bar.
Rúa de S Pedro de Alcântara. Tel: 21 347 5707.
From here you can head back down to the Baixa metro station or continue up the street to the Elevador da Glória on the right, which will take you back down to Praça dos Restauradores.

The neoclassical façade of the Teatro Nacional de São Carlos

Built on seven hills, Castelo, Graça, Monte, Penha de França, São Pedro de Alcântara, Santa Catarina and Estrela, Lisbon has numerous *miradouros* or belvederes where people come to view the city and the River Tagus.

Miradouro do Castelo

From inside the grounds of the São Jorge Castle, there are various viewing points, from the Praça de Armas just inside the castle gate to the castle walls. From here you can see the Baixa, the Chiado and the ruins of the Convento do Carmo, the domes of Santa Engrácia and the Basilica da Estrela at Amoreiras, up to the Parque Eduardo VII and the Tejo.
Trams: 12 & 28.

Miradouro da Graça

On the other side of the Castelo from Portas do Sol is the typical district of Graça. The Largo Graça offers a splendid view looking towards the castle, the River Tagus and the Basilica da Estrela, and the rooftops of the Mouraria, the Baixa, the Miradouro de São Pedro de Alcântara, the Convento do Carmo, Jardim Botânico and the Parque Eduardo VII. Relax here in the shade of the pine trees.
Tram: 18.

Miradouro at Largo Penha de França

Located just east of Estefánia district, the Largo Penha de França has a great panoramic view of the Tagus Valley with a glimpse of the Atlantic in the distance. To the east, you can see the Cemeterio do Alto de São João and on towards the river, while the northern view looks towards the Serra de Sintra. *Bus: 107.*

Miradouros at Largo Portas do Sol and Largo Santa Luzia

Both located just below the Miradouro do Castelo, from the Largo Portas do Sol and the Largo Santa Luzia you get a good view of the Igreja de São Vicente de Fora, and over the rooftops of the old Alfama district and the River Tagus. Santa Luzia also has a café, and *azulejos* showing Lisbon before the earthquake.
Trams: 28 & 12. Bus: 37.

Miradouro de Santa Catarina

Located in the Bairro Alto towards Estrela, the Miradouro de Santa Catarina offers views of the banks of the River Tagus. Set in a green square, it looks over the roofs towards the ports. To the east lies the Basílica da Estrela and in the west the districts of Lapa and Madragoa.
Tram: 28. Buses: 15 & 100.

Miradouro de São Pedro de Alcântara

This belvedere is set in a pretty shaded park, looking over the Baixa and the Avenida da Liberdade towards the Parque Eduardo VII and the districts of northern Lisbon. It also has a great view of the Castelo de São Jorge, and is a great place to rest if you have just walked up the hill. *Lift: Elevador da Glória.*

These are just a few of the best belvederes, but there are numerous others including the Largo Santo Estevão, the Parque Eduardo VII and the Travessa Torel, located at the top of the Elevador da Lavra. Other views not to be missed are: from the top of the Padrão dos Descobrimentos and the Torre de Belém, which both offer great views over the River Tagus and Belém (there is a lift to the top of the Padrão but you have to walk up quite a few steps to get to the top of the Torre); and the Torre Vasco da Gama, which looks over the Parque das Nações and the Ponte Vasco da Gama as it worms its way across the River Tagus (there is a lift up here too).

Above: The Miradouro de São Pedro de Alcântara looks towards the castle

Parque das Nações (Nation's Park)

Originally built for Expo '98, the Parque das Nações is a showpiece of modern architecture that pushes Lisbon towards the future while still reflecting its rich history.

Torre Vasco da Gama

Lying along a 5km (3 mile) stretch of the River Tagus in the northeast of the city, the architectural style is totally modern. The airport is ten minutes by taxi or local bus, and local and national trains run into Oriente Station. The station is worth seeing, with its metal and glass roof resembling palm trees. Every Sunday there are markets here, and there is a bus station outside and parking facilities below the Vasco da Gama shopping centre next door. Avoid going at the weekend when the mall gets very busy.

When you emerge from the front of the shopping centre, you are hit by the sensation of space and light. In contrast to the packed centre of Lisbon, the Parque das Nações is clean, spacious and flat. There are no hills here but there is a cable car which takes you from the Oceanarium to the Vasco da Gama Tower.

The Oceanarium is the largest in Europe, with 10,000 animals and plants from 350 species. A central tank spans two floors and represents the open sea with sharks, stingrays and groupers, amongst others, just centimetres from your face. Branching off from this tank are the Antarctic, Atlantic, Pacific and Indian Oceans, with the top floor representing life above water and the lower floor life underwater.

The Vasco da Gama Tower at the other end of the cable car ride was the emblem of Expo '98. From the viewing tower, 105m (345ft) up in the air, not only can you see over the whole area and the Vasco da Gama Bridge, but you realise that it represents the crow's nest of a boat with the deck down below.

In between these structures there is a Virtual Reality Pavilion with the latest visual technologies – the Pavilhão Atlântico. This hosts all kinds of entertainment from concerts to international sports contests, and the Teatro Camões that has brought internationally renowned theatre and dance companies to the park. The park boasts a large exhibition centre, the Feira Internacional de Lisboa, at over 100,000m^2 (1,076,000 sq ft). As if this was not enough, the Pavilhão do Conhecimento (Knowledge Pavilion) presents a series of science and technology exhibitions throughout the year, and cultural exhibitions are shown in various places around the park.

Other kinds of entertainment and leisure opportunities range from the multiplex cinema in the shopping centre to bowling, boating and bike hire. Restaurants line the riverfront and the plazas, with food available from burgers to Brazilian brasseries (*rodizio*). There are open spaces, parks and sculptures in between everything, and even a tourist train to get you around. You might not have the kind of experience here that you expect from Lisbon, but you can definitely spend an enjoyable day here.

The Oceanarium is the largest in Europe

Walk: Parque das Nações

This circular walk takes you round on a whistle-stop tour of this modern Lisbon development through the ultra-modern 'invented city' of Parque das Nações. Built specifically for Expo '98, the area is a showcase of modern architecture, and this walk passes some of the best works from Siza's Portuguese Pavilion and the Oceanário to the Torre Vasco da Gama via a cable car that offers fantastic views of both the 'park' and the River Tejo (Tagus).
Allow 2 hours.

Start at Oriente Metro. Walk out of the station and through Shopping Vasco da | *Gama. Cross the road and turn right around the Doca dos Olivais (Olivais Dock).*

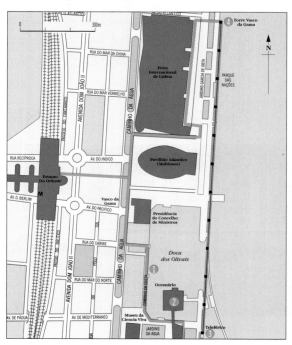

NATION'S PARK CARD

The *Cartão do Parque* saves money on many attractions around the park. You will have free entrance to the Oceanarium for a start, for a little more than the cost of the entrance fee, and in addition the Torre Vasco da Gama, the cable car and the little yellow excursion train are thrown in for nothing. Discounts are available on the other pavilions as well as the restaurants. You can buy the card at the Oceanarium, the Vasco da Gama Tower, the Nation's Park Information Desk, the Lisbon Tourism Offices / Welcome Centres and the Tivoli Tejo Hotel. Before you use the card it must be validated.
cartaodoparque@parqued asnacoes.pt

1 Doca dos Olivais

On the right you will pass a large white building that was designed by Alvaro Siza to be the Portuguese Pavilion. In the centre is an open area where speeches were made during the Expo, with a unique curved roof that is an architectural wonder. In the closed dock there is a water sports club where you can canoe, windsurf or sail.

Turn left at the corner of the dock and walk past the Museu da Ciencia Viva, past the Jardins da Agua.

2 Oceanário (Oceanarium)

You enter the Oceanarium from the south side of the dock by going up the ramp. Whether you want to see sharks and stingrays, puffins and cute sea otters or dragon fish and jellyfish, this is a definite must-see for all ages. Take the plunge (not literally) with what may seem a steep admission charge in comparison to other tickets.

Esplanada D Carlos I – Doca dos Olivais. Tel: 21 891 7002.
Either take a detour to the Knowledge and Virtual Reality Pavilions to the right and ahead, or turn left out of the Oceanarium where you will see the cable car.

3 Teleférico (Cable Car)

As long as you are not afraid of heights, the cable car will give you a bird's-eye view over the park, passing the Pavilhão Atlântico, the huge Exhibition Centre and restaurants, as well as the Vasco da Gama Bridge.

4 Torre Vasco da Gama

Once you get off the cable car, continue walking to the end of the gardens to the Vasco da Gama Tower. You can pay to go to the top of the tower for another view of the park and a better one of the bridge. The 17km (10.5 mile) long Vasco da Gama Bridge, with 12km (7.5 miles) waving across the river, bends side to side as well as up and down to cope with the currents. *Tel: 21 896 9869.*
Once you come back down from the tower, you can either take the tourist train to the station or walk through the Jardins Garcia de Orta and alongside the exhibition centre, where you will find a good selection of restaurants and bars (see pp163–71). By turning right at the end of the exhibition centre, past the Atlantic Pavilion and across the road, you will find yourself back at the Vasco da Gama shopping centre.

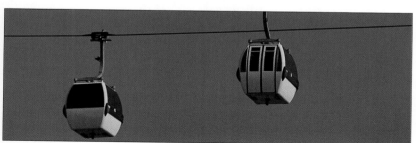

The cable car offers great views over the Parque das Nações

Alvaro Siza

In the past 20 years or so there has been an upsurge of modernisation in Portugal, particularly since 1986 when the country joined the European Union. Apart from functional infrastructure, Portugal was now setting an example in Europe in the arts. In architecture one figure has stood out: Alvaro Siza.

Born just outside Porto in Matosinhos in 1933, Siza studied architecture at the University of Porto. By the end of his studies he had already completed his first professional architectural project. Since then he has gone on to become an internationally acclaimed and multi-award winning architect and an academic, acting as visiting lecturer in Lausanne, Pennsylvania and Harvard, and holding a permanent post in Porto.

Siza has worked on projects throughout Europe. His Portuguese designs include the School of Architecture at the University of Porto, Aveiro's University Library, Setúbal College, the Museu de Arte Contemporânea at the Fundação Serralves, the Igreja de Santa Maria in Marco de Canaveses and the Portuguese pavilion at Expo '98 in Lisbon in addition to several buildings in the Chiado district of Lisbon, which was destroyed by a fire in 1988. Overseas projects include the Galicia Museum of Contemporary Art in Spain (1989–95) and the Doedijnstraat Housing Estate in The Netherlands (1989–93).

Siza has a particular style, creating large airy spaces that exude a sense of calm. More than functional, the buildings seem clean and perfect. Far from cold and stark, they draw you in. The fact that Siza attends to the details of the buildings creates a feeling of completeness. A good example of this is the Museu de Arte Contemporânea in Porto, which opened in 1999. The inside of the building blends well with its function of exhibiting modern art. The stark white walls enhance the art inside and both contrast and reflect the green of the garden outside.

One of Siza's most important projects in the last few years has been the restoration of the Chiado district in Lisbon, just close to the ruins of the Carmo convent. He has also been

working to safeguard this monument which, having all but survived the earthquake in 1755, was also weakened by the construction underground of a new metro link.

Also in Lisbon is Siza's architectural masterpiece, the Portuguese Pavilion for Expo '98 in the Parque das Nações. Located by the Doca dos Olivais, the pavilion had an open-air space for the inaugural speech and other events. In order to protect the delegates from rain it was decided to fit a cover. What Siza created was a breathtaking feat of engineering. The roof appears to be like a cloth of concrete draped over the top, and won acclaim worldwide.

All of Siza's projects are special, and they are not exclusive to a particular section of society. His projects range from buildings that are cultural, educational or functional; a museum, a university or a regeneration project.

There is no doubt that Siza has gone a long way to creating new, modern urban spaces in Portugal. Wherever his buildings are constructed, in an old or new area, they fit in with their surroundings and have a kind of architectural ergonomics.

Facing page: Museu Contemporânea de Serralves, Porto
Above: Portuguese Pavilion in Parque das Nações, Lisbon

Excursions from Lisbon

Abrantes

Located northeast of Lisbon on the north banks of the River Tagus, Abrantes is a pretty town with narrow streets, white houses, flowers and palm trees. Once an important town during the Reconquest, in the past few years reconstructive work has taken place in its historic centre and various squares and streets. There is an old **Forteza** (fortress) overlooking the town and today you can visit the archaeology museum, the **Museu Dom Lopo de Almeida**, inside the walls.

Located about 150km (93 miles) northeast of Lisbon along the A1-IP1 and IP6. Trains: leave every hour from Lisbon, most change in Entroncamento and take approximately 1³/₄ hours.
Museum: Rua Capitão Correia de Lacerda. Open: daily.

Evora

This old Roman town in the Alentejo is quite a way from Lisbon but its historical interest may persuade you to take the trip. An old Roman town, it was also occupied by the Moors, and there is still evidence of both. Parts of the **Moorish walls** surround the historic centre and ruins of the **Templo Romano** can still be seen. Other sights worth seeing are the **Sé Catedral**, the **Museu de Evora** and various churches, the old university and the 16th-century aqueduct.

Largo do Conde de Vila Flor. Tel: 26 670 2604. Open: Tue–Sun 9.30am–12.30pm & 2–6pm; closed Mon.

Located around 130km (80 miles) east-southeast of Lisbon along the A2-IP1 and A6-IP7.

City Walls

The walls that surround the town date from different periods, some from as far back as the Romans in the 1st century and the Moorish occupation (pre-12th century). While parts of the walls have collapsed, the largest remaining section is medieval and others were built in the 17th century.

Museu de Evora

Located in an old 16th-century palace next to the cathedral, the museum has a collection of ruins and relics from around the city, dating from the Romans to the Moors, and paintings by Flemish and Portuguese artists.

Largo do Conde de Vila Flor. Open: Tue–Sun 10am–12.30pm & 2–5.30pm.

Sé Catedral

Built in the 12th and 13th centuries, this fortress-like cathedral is a mixture of Romanesque and Gothic architecture. Look out for the portal with sculptures of the apostles, the cloisters (added in the 14th century) and the sacred art collection in the treasury.

Largo do Marquês de Marialva.
Open: Tue–Sun 9am–noon & 2–5pm.

Templo Romano

The well-preserved Roman Temple dates back to around the 2nd century

Templo Romano

and is thought to have been dedicated to the goddess Diana. Fourteen columns still stand round the old temple, which was used for several different functions before being rescued in the 19th century. *Largo do Conde de Vila Flor. Open: permanently.*

ople travel
ndreds of miles
come to the
silica at Fátima

Fátima
The **Basilica** at Fátima lies on the site where three children saw a vision of the Virgin at the beginning of the 20th century. Today it attracts over 4 million pilgrims every year, particularly on the 13 May and 13 October, commemorating the days when the apparition took place. There are leather kneepads for hire for those who want to prostrate themselves as they approach the shrine, and numerous shops around sell gifts. *www.santuario-fatima.pt. Located about 120km (74.5 miles) north of Lisbon along the A1-IP1, turn off just before Leiria.*

Santarém
The old Roman city of Santarém is located on the banks of the River Tagus, northeast of Santarém. There are several interesting churches, including the **Igreja e Claustro do Convento de São Francisco**, dating from the 13th–15th centuries, with Gothic, Baroque and *Manuelino* architecture. The **Igreja de Marvila** dates back further, to the 12th century, but had extensive *Manuelino* reconstruction work in the 16th century, and the

18th century saw the addition of gilded woodcarving (*Largo do Alcáçova; tel: 24 332 5552*). The **Jardim das Portas do Sol** are also worth a visit, with a garden, aviary and fantastic viewing point over the River Tagus (*Largo do Alcáçova; tel: 24 332 5552*). Today the city is particularly renowned for its agricultural fair and bullfights in June.
Located around 75km (47 miles) northeast of Lisbon along the A1-IP1. Trains: two or three an hour from Lisbon's Oriente Station, they take less than an hour.

Setúbal

Portugal's third-largest port town, Setúbal is an interesting place and a stopping point if going further south, to the nearby beaches or parks.

Igreja de Jesus

This Gothic church was built by Diego Boitac in 1494 and is one of the earliest examples of *Manuelino* architecture. See the carved rope-like decoration and the pink columns made from local Arrábida stone.
Praça Miguel Bombarda. Open: Tue–Sun.

Castelo de São Filipe

Built in the 16th century to defend the city from pirates, today the castle is a *pousada* where you can stay in luxury or visit the cosy bar and restaurant. There are fabulous views over the city from here.
Estrada de São Filipe. Open: daily.

Sintra

A national heritage site, Sintra is a must-see on any trip to the area

around Lisbon. Located in green hills west of Lisbon, it is full of mansions and palaces from Portugal's Romantic period and it used to be a royal summer retreat. It has been a UNESCO World Heritage Site since 1995. Top visiting spots include the **Castelo dos Mouros**, the **Palácio Nacional da Pena**, the **Palácio Nacional da Vila de Sintra**, the **Museu de Arte Moderna** and the **Museu do Brinquedo**.
Located 20km (12.5 miles) west of Lisbon along the IC19.

Castelo dos Mouros

The castle was built by the Moors in the 8th or 9th centuries, and conquered by Dom Afonso Henriques in 1147. It was rebuilt by Dom Fernando II in the 19th century, but still retains a Romanesque chapel inside. Today it has been transformed into a hotel.
Estrada da Pena. Open: daily.

Museu de Arte Moderna

Sintra's modern art museum is located in a beautiful mansion that also used to be a casino. It has an important collection of European and American art, including some of the most famous works from the 20th century.
Avenida Heliodoro Salgado. Tel: 21 924 8170. Open: Wed–Sun 10am–6pm & Tue 2–6pm.

Museu do Brinquedo

This fabulous toy museum has about 20,000 pieces from various historical periods that range from lead soldiers to electric trains, dolls and dinky toys.
Largo Latino Coelho. Open: Tue–Sun 10am–6pm.

Sintra is a UNESCO World Heritage Site and should not be missed

Palácio Nacional da Mafra

Located in the town of Mafra, northwest of Lisbon, this palace consists of a **basilica**, **convent** and **palace** and is considered one of the most important examples of Portuguese Baroque architecture. It was built by Dom João V following a vow to God wishing that a son be born to him, and took 27 years to construct (1717–44). In addition to signs of Portuguese, German and Italian Baroque, the palace has a 200m (656ft) façade, 114 bells and a library of classical works, thought to be one of the most beautiful in the world. As the royal family's old official summer residence, the sumptuous building and grounds were used for hunting and leisure. It is surrounded by the woods and gardens of the Jardim do Cerco garden and the Tapada Real park, the old palace hunting ground.
Mafra is located about 25km (15.5 miles) northwest of Lisbon along the N117 and N9. Palace: Terreiro de Dom João V. Open: Wed–Mon 10am–1pm & 2–5.30pm.

Palácio Nacional da Pena

Overlooking Sintra, this is a fairytale palace and one of the most important and modern examples of Portugal's architectural heritage. It was built on the orders of the prince consort Dom Fernando II in the mid-19th century on top of ruins of an Hieronymite monastery destroyed by the Great Earthquake in 1755. The palace is eclectic in style ranging from *mudéjar* to *Manuelino*, and it retains Fernando's collections of decorative art. The old convent church has a *Manuelino* bossed vault and walls covered in blue and white *azulejos*.
Palácio Nacional da Pena, 2710, Sintra. Open: Tue–Sun 10am–1pm & 2–6.30pm. Buses run frequently from the city centre and take 20 minutes.

Palácio Nacional da Vila de Sintra

As well as being Portugal's only intact medieval royal palace, the Palácio Nacional boasts the country's largest example of tile work. Originally built in the 14th century, it has since had several extensions and it is an amalgamation of Gothic, *Manuelino* and *mudéjar* architecture. Look out for the two huge Gothic cone-shaped chimneys and the east wing, built during the reign of Dom Manuel I, which has a coat of arms with *mudéjar* decoration. Today the palace is often used for official banquets.
Largo Rainha Dona Amélia. Open: Thur–Tue 10am–1pm & 2–5pm.

Palácio Nacional de Queluz

Often regarded as the most attractive royal residence from the Age of Enlightenment (1747–86), the pink Palácio Nacional de Queluz has a garden named after one of the statues, Jardim de Neptuno, and a Robillon façade named after the architect who designed it. One of the best rooms is the Sala do Trono (Throne Room), with a domed ceiling and wood-carved walls. You can also eat in the Cozinha Velha, the old palace kitchen, which has been converted into a luxury restaurant.
Located a few miles from Sintra along the N249. Trains: leave from Lisbon's Rossio station. Palace: signposted from station.

The faded opulence of the Palácio de Queluz

Getting Away from it All

After a few days wandering around the sites of Lisbon, you might want something more sedate. As well as relaxing in one of the city parks, having a round of golf or taking a river trip, there are beaches, natural parks and wine routes all within an hour's drive.

Sailing on the Tejo

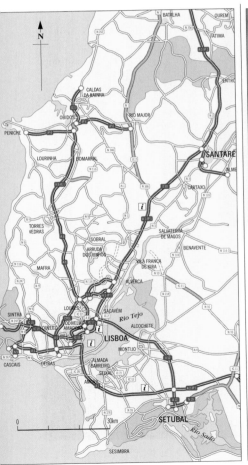

Golf course at Aoreira near Lisbon

Belavista Golf Course

Designed by António Barnabé and opened in 2002, this golf course is located in central Lisbon. A nine-hole, 32-par course, it is great for those who want to escape the city streets for a while.
Avenida Avelino Teixeira da Mota.
Tel: 21 831 0860.

Costa da Caparica

Lying between the River Tagus estuary and the Cabo Espichel on the Setúbal peninsular, the Costa da Caparica has

over 13km (8 miles) of sandy beaches, including Fonte da Telha, Meco and Lagoa de Albufeira. From the Cabo towards Setúbal there are more beaches, all south facing, and on the south bank of the River Sado is Tróia, a great sandy peninsular.
Located south of Lisbon across the Ponte 25 de Abril, then bear right to the coast.

Jardim Botánico
Set in the heart of Lisbon, this botanical garden (*see p44*) is a great way to escape. You can forget about the sounds of the city and listen to the birds instead!

Parque Florestal do Monsanto
The largest green area of Lisbon (*see p43*), this park has a wealth of animal and plant life, and facilities for sports, children's games and bird watching.

Parque Natural da Arrábida
Just west of the city of Setúbal, this large natural park boasts beautiful landscape and rare flora. You can drive round a large proportion of the park amongst the pines and privets, Californian pepper trees and dwarf palms, and forests of oak trees. As well as three botanical and natural parks, there is a wildlife park on the Ilhéu da Pedra da Anixa in the cove of Portinho da Arrábida beach, Roman ruins at Creiro, a cave with a chapel inside close to Portinho and the fortress here, the Forte de Nossa Senhora da Arrábida. You can also visit the Cabo Espichel, which is an area of preserved cliffs and fells where

dinosaur remains have been found, the Museu Oceanográfico in the Fortaleza de Santa Maria at Arrábida and the Reserva Botânica das Dunas de Troia.
Located south of Lisbon along the A2-IP1. The tourist office has more information on tours and hiking routes.
Posto de Turismo, Castelo de Palmela. Tel: 21 233 2122.

Parque Natural de Sintra-Cascais
Located west of Lisbon, this large natural park runs through sand dunes, gardens and forests. You can take some interesting walks around here, including from the Palácio da Vila to the Parque da Pena in Sintra, while the Cabo da Roca is the most westerly point in Europe. Walk in the gardens of the palace at Monserrate or head for one of the beaches at Samarra, Magoito, Azenhas do Mar, Praia Grande, Praia das Maçãs and Adraga. You can also follow the trail of dinosaurs in the Jazida de Carenque

Village in Serra da Arrábida

close to Belas.

Located west of Lisbon along the A5. Contact the tourist office for trails and routes. Junta de Turismo de Costa do Estoril, Arcadas do Parque 2769–503, Estoril. Tel: 21 466 3813/21 468 7044.

Reserva Natural do Estuário do Tejo

Upriver from the city of Lisbon, close to the Ponte Vasco da Gama, this is the largest aquatic reserve in Portugal, with more than 45,000 hectares (111,195 acres) of protected landscape. Its marshes attract migratory birds and fish, and there is a colony of 6,000 flamingos.

Located upriver by the Ponte Vasco da Gama. There are boat tours. See below for information.

River Trips on the Tagus

There is a special Transtejo boat that offers two-hour sightseeing trips along the city's riverbanks between Parque das Nações and Belém, with departures from the ferry station in Terreiro do Paço (Praça do Comércio).

The ferry operator also offers three special excursion trips leaving from the Cais do Sodré. The first takes you up the estuary to see the flamingos in the natural reserve, the second tours the reserve as

Sailing – the perfect pursuit for relaxation

far as the riverbank stilt houses, and the third cruises upriver to Almourol Castle and the town of Constância (or further, if you like, to the Belver Dam).

There are numerous regular ferry routes on the River Tagus, which you can use either as a relaxing way to get away or as a means of transport to get to the south side of the estuary.
Transtejo, tel: 21 882 0348. Cruises, tel: 26 553 7580.

Wine Routes

A delicious way to get away from it all, wine routes are in abundance around Lisbon. The closest to the city are west at Carcavelos and Colares, south at the Quinta do Anjo, Palmela and Azeitão and north at Bucelas, Arruda dos Vinhos, Turcifal and Sobral de Mte Agraço. However, there are more depending on how far you want to stray from the city. You can visit vineyards and cellars and appreciate some of the local wines. There are also fairs held at Cataxo and Alpiarça.

The tourist office has a full list of places that offer tours and how to get to each one. Welcome Center, Loja 2–10, 1-r/c, Praça do Comércio, Lisbon; tel: 21 031 2815 or Palácio Foz, Praça dos Restauradores, Lisbon; tel: 21 346 3314.

The River Tagus ferry

Porto: Introduction

There are various images associated with Porto. Overseas it is known for its Port wine, while in Lisbon its people are referred to as *tripeiros*, or tripe eaters. It has also been called a 'city of bridges', reflecting its position on trade routes and the need to fill the gap between its past and future.

Porto's Torre dos Clérigos is a good meeting-point

Porto started out as a Roman trading post on the road to Lisbon, and by the 14th century, it had become the focal point for mercantile activity. Its population grew, with the city walls spreading out in all directions.

The first main period of expansion in Porto occurred in the 12th century when a large area was given to the bishop Dom Hugo. Under the jurisdiction of the clergy, the city developed as a city for the *povo*, the people. There were always conflicts between the nobility and the clergy. At one point, noblemen were only allowed to stay in the city for a maximum of three days. Perhaps this early history goes some way to explain why Porto was loyal to the Portuguese royal family against the Castilians (1383), but backed

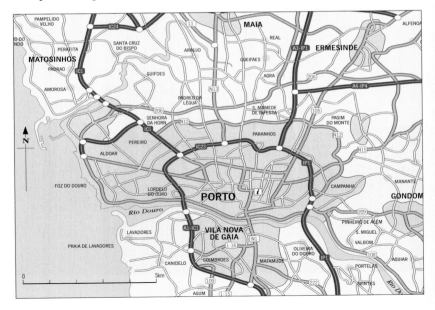

the liberal causes rather than the authoritarian ones whenever there was internal struggle.

As with other parts of the country, the Age of Discoveries was an important part of Porto's social and cultural psyche. The first, and one of the most famous names in this era, the Infante Dom Henrique, or Henry the Navigator, was born in Porto and from there set sail for the conquest of Ceuta in 1415. Because of Henry, the *portuenses* (people of Porto), earned their name of *tripeiros*, as they gave him the good meat, leaving only the tripe for themselves. Even today, *tripa à moda de Porto* is a local traditional dish, although possibly more popular in the poorer areas of the city.

Although Port wine has been produced for near on two millennia, exports rose from the 17th century mainly due to foreign wine merchants, particularly the British, who were then given special trade concessions in the 18th century.

The city has seen periods of prosperity and growth, but it has also suffered destruction, disease and poverty due to wars, from the wars of accession to the Napoleonic, and even World Wars I and II. Reconstruction and redevelopment has taken place sporadically, medieval buildings intersperse with Baroque and neo-classical ones in the old city centre, a UNESCO World Heritage Site since 1996. However, little was known abroad about the city beyond its association with Port wine.

After Portugal joined the European Union in 1986, Porto started to emerge from the mist that had so long shrouded it. New bridges and roads were built along with state-of-the-art shopping centres and modern museums. Not only is Porto more accessible to the country, the expansion of the airport and its 2001 status as European City of Culture have gone a long way to showing Porto's cultural face to the rest of the world. Modernisation continues in the city as it firmly walks into the new millennium, protecting its past and assuring its place in the future.

The traditional rabelo boats once carried the Port barrels downriver from the Douro Valley

Porto: City

Porto lies 41°8' north, and 8°36' west, sitting on the River Douro looking out towards the Atlantic Ocean. The city of Porto stretches along the north bank of the river with 45km² (17 sq miles) of conurbation in total, and a population of around 300,000. On the south bank of the River Douro, lies Vila Nova de Gaia, officially another city but so close it feels part of Porto. The metropolitan area of Porto measures 817km² (315 sq miles) with a population of over 1.15 million.

The famous Sandeman logo stands atop the Port wine house

View of Porto's Ribeira district from Vila Nova de Gaia

Porto is the capital of the north of Portugal and its second largest city. With its location at the mouth of the River Douro, Porto developed as a commerce centre for goods, particularly wine from the Douro region, a trade and transport route to Lisbon and the rest of Europe.

The first permanent bridge across the river, however, was not built until the beginning of the 19th century and it was then destroyed by the Napoleonic invasions. Once the war ended, Porto expanded with the need for more road and rail bridges. Since 1986, when the country joined the European Union, the city has seen rapid improvement of motorways and bypasses, facilitating travel to and from other important commercial centres in the country.

Areas of Porto

Officially Porto is divided into 15 districts: São Nicolau, Sé, Vitória, Miragaia, Cedofeita, Massarelos and Santo Ildefonso in the centre; Bonfim, Campanhã and Paranhos in the east; and Ramalde, Lordelo do Ouro, Foz do Douro, Aldoar and Novogilde in the west. However, within these some areas have popular names, such as the Ribeira, the historic area by the Douro, in the district of São Nicolau.

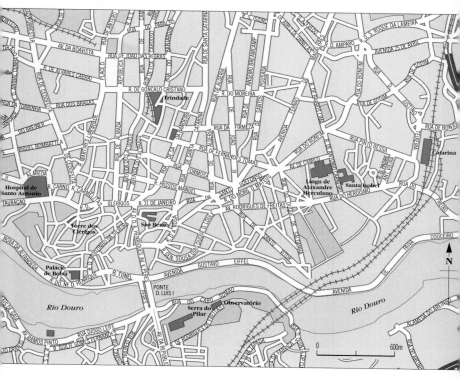

The first part of the city was built on the hill around the Sé Catedral, and it expanded outwards from here. Located just west of the Dom Luís I bridge, the narrow streets of the Sé lead downhill to the Ribeira an ancient district with a mixture of medieval streets, lavish Baroque churches and neo-classical officialdom, including riverside restaurants, cafés and old shop fronts.

These two areas form the major part of the city's UNESCO World Heritage Site.

Just north of the Ribeira and Sé is the Baixa – old downtown with the Praça da Liberdade and the Avenida dos Aliados. The roads climb up from here to the pedestrian shopping area of Santa Catarina in the east, the municipal buildings in the Praça da República to

View along Avenida Boavista, which runs to the Atlantic Coast

the north, the Rua da Restauração to the west, which leads back down to the riverside, and the medieval church of Cedofeita in the northwest. These areas form the traditional old downtown areas of Porto.

On the south side of the River Douro, you can see the city of Vila Nova de Gaia, home to the Port wine lodges that are the reason for much of Porto's fame.

One of the main arteries of the city is Boavista which runs just west of the centre to the Atlantic coast by the port of Matosinhos. Just south of here is Foz do Douro, a pretty residential area with a castle, wide esplanades and a road that runs upriver and northwards along the coast.

A circular road leads from the Ponte da Arrábida across Boavista and around the downtown area, passing the principal railway station, Campanhã, in the east and back down across the river over the Ponte do Freixo. A wide bypass, the Estrada da Circunvalação, runs from just north of the Ponte do Freixo around the northern part of the city and west to Matosinhos. These roads are useful for navigating from one side of the city to the other, and form connecting roads to Vila Nova de Gaia, Lisbon, Guimarães, Braga and the airport.

Climate

Porto's climate is influenced by its riverside location, the closeness to the Atlantic and the hills inland. The average summer temperature is around 18.5°C (May–September), but it can get much hotter than this. However, the afternoons can be windy as breezes come in from the ocean. In the winter (November–March), the average temperature is 10.5°C but it can be wet and misty, with the occasional mild day thrown in.

Henry the Navigator

Born in 1394 in Porto in what became known as the Casa do Infante, Henry the Navigator (Infante D Henrique) was the son of the King D João I and Philippa of Lancaster, and became a legendary figure.

From Porto he led the Portuguese army on the Conquest of Céuta, a Muslim stronghold in Morocco. Here he saw evidence of the riches to be had in the rest of Africa and his ambitions of conquest, Christianisation, geographic knowledge and trade grew.

In 1420 the Pope named him Governor of the Order of Christ and he pursued his aims as a crusader as much as a discoverer, seeking to gain victory over the Muslims. A scientific man, skilled in navigation, he set up his own school of navigation in Sagres, and from here new maps were created and the *caravela* ship was developed.

From 1424–34 Henry the Navigator sent out 15 expeditions, but none of them dared go beyond Cape Bojador, just south of the Canaries. Suspicion about the edge of the world still reigned, and the sailors feared the deep waters. Eventually he persuaded Gil Eannes to make a second attempt and this time he conquered his fears.

After this, the expeditions proceeded further south, and by the time he died in 1460, the Portuguese had increased trade and reached Liberia and the Cape Verde Islands.

History

5th century BC	The south bank of the River Douro is called Cale, and the north side Portus, later known collectively as Portus Cale and Portucale.
AD 711	Moors disembark in Gibraltar and eventually reach the Douro and Braga.
868	Count Vímara Peres from Galicia retakes northern Portugal from the Moors, re-Christianising and reorganising the city around the Sé hill.
1120	Dona Teresa concedes a large area to the bishop Dom Hugo. Rapid development takes place and the city walls are extended.
1330	Porto is the focal point of mercantile activity.
mid-14th century	A new city wall is constructed to protect the city from enemies as it grows.
1355	Infante Dom Pedro unsuccessfully tries to depose his father, Dom Alfonso IV, but accedes to the throne in 1357.
	He decides to build new city walls, but these remain unfinished until the reign of Dom Fernando.
1383–5	Porto takes the side of the leader of the House of Avis, Dom João I, against the Castilians.
1394	Henry the Navigator is born in Porto.
1415	Henry the Navigator forms part of the expedition that conquers Ceuta.
15th century	The city now has three basic areas: Alta (the Sé, centre of ecclesiastical power), Baixa (the Ribeira, home to fishers and market traders) and the Monte do Olival (the Jewish quarter).
14th–15th centuries	The Age of Discoveries leads to circulation of 'exotic' goods, the city grows, the road network improves and newer larger squares are built. This period also saw the *autos-da-fé* (the burning of heretics by Christians).
1580	The population of Porto suffers 60 years of occupation by Felipe I (Phillip II of Spain).

17th century	Porto grows due to the development of the Port wine industry.	**1851–86**	The city sees slow regeneration, but it is politically unstable.
1703	Menthuen Treaty favours the export of wines to Great Britain. Foreign influence in the city grows.	**1886**	Strikes against foreign employers rise along with political discontent. On 31 January a group of republican soldiers revolt but are crushed by royalists.
18th century	Nicolau Nasoni builds Baroque buildings such as the Torre dos Clérigos and the facade of the Igreja da Misericórdia.	**1899**	The city elects three republican deputies.
First half of 19th century	Revolts, plague and starvation leave the city in ruins.	**1961**	Colonial wars start. Various demonstrations are organised in Porto.
1807	Hundreds drown as they flee across the river from Napoleonic troops.	**1974**	Restoration of democracy following the Carnation Revolution leads to reactionary movements in Porto.
1811	The French are expelled from the country by the English. Dom João returns to the Portuguese throne.	**1996**	Porto declared a UNESCO World Heritage Site.
1822	Even though Dom Pedro IV gives the people a new Constitution, upheaval and war are inevitable.	**2001**	Porto celebrates its status as European City of Culture.
Second half of 19th century	The Industrial Revolution sees new factories, bourgeoisie neighbourhoods and avenues. Rise of textile, clothing, food and drink industries.		

Porto's most famous son, Prince Henry the Navigator, stands aloft in the square named after him

Culture and Festivals in Porto

Porto is not known for its cultural output or lively atmosphere, rather it is seen as a mercantile city where the people work hard and leave the partying to Lisbon. However, it has architecture to rival any other city and is now pushing forward into the new millennium with new buildings, cultural centres, theatre and music.

Igreja de São Nicolau

NICOLAU NASONI

Born in Tuscany in 1691, Nicolau Nasoni came to Porto in 1725 and left an indelible mark on the city with his prized pieces of architecture. An architect, sculptor and painter, he started work on the Torre dos Clérigos in 1731 and completed it in 1763. His other works in the city include the design of the silver altar and wooden staircase in the Sé Catedral, the renovation of the façade of the Igreja da Miseracórdia and the Capela-mor in the Igreja de Santo Ildefonso amongst the Palácio do Freixo. He died in apparent poverty in 1773 and was interred in the Igreja dos Clérigos in an unmarked tomb.

Art and Architecture

The UNESCO World Heritage Site in Porto is a rich array of architecture, with Roman ruins buried under the medieval settlement of Sé (*see pp110–11*). As the city grew from the takings of the Discoveries and then from the growth of the Port wine industry, Porto became a showcase of elaborate Baroque architecture, particularly its churches. Later the

Porto's tightly-packed Ribeira district

There has always been plenty of foreign influence in Porto

influence of the British became apparent with the more sober and functional neo-classical buildings such as the Palácio da Bolsa.

Having suffered numerous wars, disease and poverty, Porto can seem 'grey' in comparison to Lisbon, but the longer you stay the more interesting it becomes. Medieval sits next to Baroque, and neo-classical, gilded woodcarvings and elaborate *azulejos* cover the walls and churches, cloisters and stations. There are many hidden treasures. For example, behind the neo-classical facade of the Bolsa, the rooms are elaborately decorated in Moorish and imperial styles, with frescos by António Ramalho and paintings by António Carneiro, both renowned artists in their field.

During the 1960s, Porto artists were at the forefront of avant-garde expression, particularly in the Cooperativa Arvore, where they spoke out against the repression of the dictatorship.

Founded in 1963 by a group of artists who wanted freedom of expression, the cooperative struggled and even after the revolution in 1974 there were upheavals, culminating in it being bombed in 1976. However it survived, now, after more than 40 years, it has become legendary.

More recently, Porto has pulled itself into the 21st century with the country's best contemporary architect, Alvaro Siza, leading the way with the construction of buildings such as the Faculty of Architecture and the Museu de Arte Contemporânea (*see pp74–5*). This has boosted Porto's art scene and its general profile. Numerous modern centres have encouraged the culture of

Almeida Garrett Library, built as part of Porto's European Capital of Culture celebrations

window shopping at weekends and brought multiplex cinemas, fast food and fashion to the masses.

Music and Theatre

While popular culture is booming, more traditional theatres present events of both high and low culture. The Teatro Nacional de São João, the Rivoli and the Coliseu present everything from orchestral concerts through folk and pop, to ballet and modern dance, and the odd circus.

During the early 20th century, Porto's music scene was promoted by Bernardo Valentim Moreira de Sá (1853–1924), who created a basic musical infrastructure. He founded musical groups which culminated in the formation of the Porto Music Conservatory. His son-in-law continued his work, bringing international names in music to the city.

As the 20th century progressed, other music groups were formed including the Orquestra Nacional do Porto and, more recently, the Remix Ensemble percussion group, both of which are to be housed at the Casa da Música (when it is finished), the so-called emblem of Porto 2001 (European City of Culture), which helped a great deal to further boost the city's cultural output.

Literature

The best-known figure in Porto's literature scene is 19th-century writer Almeida Garrett. During the 20th century, however, a few other figures stand out such as António Pedro, who founded and directed the Experimental Theatre of Porto.

Almeida Garrett

Born in Porto in 1799, Almeida Garrett was a poet, dramatist and journalist as well as a politician. He spent two periods in exile due to his support of the liberal cause in the revolution of 1820. On his return in 1832, he became the leading Romantic writer in Portugal but did not abandon his political career, becoming a democrat. His published works include *Flores sem fruto* (1844), *Fôlhas caídas* (1853) and *Viagems na minha terra* (1846). The city of Porto pays homage to Garrett with monuments, roads and

Watch out for flying vegetables at the Festas de São João

even a new library named after him. The tourist office has also designed a tour to help you to get to know the writer better.

Festivals in Porto

Porto is now developing its cultural output and increasing the number of festivals and events it holds, particularly since Porto 2001. However, the **Festas de São João** have been celebrated for a long time. Held in June to honour the city's saint, people wave around garlic, leeks and basil, jump over fires and bang each other on the head with foam 'hammers'! There is also music, dancing and fireworks.

The city also hosts various other annual festivals and events:

- In February **Fantasporto** is the country's best cinema festival with a focus on fantasy films;
- In March the **Porto Inter-Celtic Festival** presents concerts of popular music;
- April sees the **International Cartoon Festival**;
- The **FITEI International Theatre Festival** in May has 15 days of theatre from the Portuguese-speaking world;
- **Noites Rituais** in August presents the best of Portuguese rock music;
- September sees the **Porto International Piano Competition** which attracts entrants from all over the world;
- The **Porto Jazz Festival** in October and November attracts internationally renowned musicians;
- December is dedicated to the **Puppet Festival** with performances at various theatres around the city.

Impressions

When you come to the centre of Porto for the first time, it can appear grey and dirty, poor and cut off from the modern excesses of the West. Yet within the medieval alleys of the Ribeira lies a rich medieval history, one now protected by its status as a UNESCO World Heritage Site. The people are open and friendly, and willing to help the visiting public.

Stock Exchange Palace

Arriving by train is a different experience. From Spain you travel south through green vineyards and from the south you pass close to sandy beaches and golf courses before crossing the River Douro with its spectacular views of Vila Nova de Gaia and the Ribeira.

The infrastructure around Porto has come a long way since the late 1980s. Once it took hours to travel in from neighbouring cities. Cars had to pass along winding roads and local trains took their time, stopping where they pleased. Now the fast Alfa Intercity Express and motorways speed your journey into the small city, and a new metro system is being built to ease movement.

As people have moved in from the country, the city has spread outwards with high-rise apartments springing up in the outskirts. The city's status as European City of Culture in 2001 also quickened the changes, although everything in Portugal takes longer than planned. Squares have been repaved, buildings renovated, bridges erected and modern museums and cultural centres constructed.

Walk down steep steps to the riverfront and you may still get a whiff of poor Porto, but change is certainly underway and international influences are prevalent, from the heart of the old shopping district to the large shopping malls that are now so popular. Old and new exist side by side, mansions and churches with intricately painted *azulejos* sit alongside magnificent clean lines of new buildings.

Passe Porto

This is a pass for tourists that is valid for one or two days, as you choose, and gives discount or even free access to many museums and monuments. You also get free travel on the STCP transport (buses and trams), discounts in some shops, entertainments, tours, cruises and taxis. The pass can be purchased from any of the city's tourist offices: *Rua Clube Fenianos, 25; Rua do Infante D Henrique, 63; Praça D João I, 25, 4th floor.*

When to Go

It can get warm in Porto in the summer, but if you want to get out of the city and

There are still a couple of trams operating around the city

head for the beach, it is best to go in the morning. In the afternoon, there is often an onshore wind from the Atlantic. In the winter it can get cold and you will need to wrap up in your winter coat, but this is not the Arctic and there can be mild days. Rain is more prevalent from mid-September to December, so be prepared to take cover.

Getting Around
Walking is the best way to explore the historic centre of Porto with its cobbled streets and steps, but to go further you can make use of the expanding public transport system, drive or take a taxi. Detailed information on all forms of transport is available from the Mobility Shop (Loja de Mobilidad).
Rua Clube dos Fenianos, 25.
www.cm-porto.pt.

Buses
The STCP (Sociedad de Transportes Colectivos do Porto, SA) is Porto's main bus operator. During the day there are 81 routes and 40 of these run until midnight. There are also night buses on 14 routes through the main sections of the city, with connections at the Praça da Liberdade. You can buy single and multi-journey tickets, as well as one-day passes. These must be validated when you get on the bus by using the machine next to the driver. There is also an airport bus that passes the main hotels and central Porto, and other operators run routes out of the city.

Tram
STCP also runs the old tram network, which is basically two routes: the E1 from Passeio Alegre to Infante, and

route 18 from Massarelos and Viriato. Passengers have to pay the conductor or can use their one-day passes or travel cards.

Metro

Construction of the metro system in Porto is currently underway and some stations have already opened on the Blue Line at the Matosinhos end. The lines will run from central Porto to Matosinhos, Vila Nova de Gaia and Trofa. This means that some of the old rail services have been deactivated, with bus services operating in the meantime.

Trains

There is a commuter service run by Caminhos de Ferro Portugueses, EP,

which comprises four lines between Porto and cities and towns within a 60km (37 mile) radius. There are three stations in Porto: São Bento, Campanhã and Contumil. The UVIR (Unidade de Viagens Interurbanas e Regionais, CP) operates trains to several domestic and international destinations from Campanhã and São Bento. The AlfaPendular is the fast, comfortable, intercity service.

Taxis

Taxis are a reasonable way to get around and are either metered or by the hour. This has to be agreed in advance. There are taxi ranks throughout the city, details of which can be obtained from the Mobility Shop (*www.cm-porto.pt*).

Local train service

The sights are well signposted

River

The Sociedade dos Catraeiros da Douro carries people across the Douro from Cais do Ouro in Porto to Afurada in Vila Nova de Gaia. This takes about five minutes and tickets are purchased on board.

Car

Driving in Porto can be frustrating due to the amount of traffic on the roads and the different style of driving. However, there are various car parks, and shopping centres have ample spaces. Road networks to other cities have also vastly improved, facilitating journeys further afield.

Pollution in Porto

Beaches around Porto are not the best because they suffer the effects of oil tankers docking in Leça, near Matosinhos. In addition to oil, the sewage and waste is too close to the beach and pumps out of the River Douro. It is best to head further south or north for cleaner beaches. Industry and the volume of traffic affect air quality, and the pollution levels fluctuate according to season.

Museu Nacional Soares
dos Reis

Museums

For a small city, Porto has a good selection of museums,
from fine art and history to science and transport. The best
museums, though, are the Serralves Museum of
Contemporary Art and the Soares dos Reis National
Museum but the city has numerous collections that are
located in former residencies of notable figures.

Casa Museu Guerra Junqueiro (Guerra Junqueiro Museum House)

Located in an 18th-century Baroque
house designed by Nicolau Nasoni,
the museum contains important
articles belonging to the poet Guerra
Junqueiro.
*Rua de Dom Hugo, 32. Tel: 22 200 3689.
Open: Mon–Fri 10am–12.30pm &
2–5pm, Sat & Sun 2–5.30pm. Admission
charge. Buses: 3, 6 & 71.*

Casa-Oficina António Carneiro (António Carneiro's House & Office)

The museum contains a large collection
of work by Porto artist António
Carneiro (1872–1930).
*Rua António Carneiro, 363. Tel: 22 537
9668. Open: Tue–Sat 10am–12.30pm
& 2–5.30pm, Sun 2–6pm. Buses: 11,
12 & 13.*

Casa Tait (Tait House)

This museum is a treat for coin
enthusiasts with a Greek, Roman,
Hispanic, Arabian and Portuguese
collection.
*Rua de Entrequintas, 219. Open:
Mon–Fri 10am–12.30pm & 2–5.30pm,
Sat & Sun 2–5.30pm.*

Museu de Arte Contemporânea de Serralves (Serralves Museum of Contemporary Art)

*(See pp124–5.) Rua D João de Castro,
210. Tel: 22 615 6500. Open: Nov–Mar
Tue–Sun 10am–7pm (Thur until 10pm);
Apr–Oct Tue–Sun 10am–8pm
(Thur until 10pm).*

Museu do Carro Eléctrico (Tram Museum)

This museum has models of trams dating
back to the end of the 19th century.
*Alameda Basílio Teles, 51. Tel: 22 615
8185. Open: 9.30am–1pm & 3–6pm.
Admission charge. Buses: 1, 18 & 23.*

Museu dos Transportes e Comunicações (Transport and Communication Museum)

Located in the huge Customs House
building on the banks of the Douro, this
museum hosts temporary exhibitions.
*Rua Nova da Alfândega. Tel: 22 340 3000.
www.amtc.pt. Open: Tue–Fri 10am–noon
& 2–6pm, Sat & Sun, public holidays
3–7pm. Admission charge.
Buses: 1, 23 & 49.*

Museu Militar do Porto (Porto Military Museum)

There are collections of light weaponry and heavy artillery on display here dating from the 16th–20th centuries.
Rua do Heroísmo, 29. Tel: 22 236 5514. Open: Tue–Fri 10am–1pm & 2–5pm, Sat & Sun 2–5pm. Admission charge (Wed free). Buses: 35 & 80.

Museu Nacional da Imprensa (National Press Museum)

This museum was the first working museum in the country and you can still print your own articles here.
Estrada Nacional, 108, 206. Tel: 22 530 4966. Open: daily 3–8pm. Admission charge. Buses: 80 & 88.

Museu Nacional Soares dos Reis (Soares dos Reis National Museum)

Located in an 18th-century neo-classical palace, the museum was renovated and extended for the city's European City of Culture celebrations in 2001. The permanent collection includes Portuguese painters and sculptors, particularly Silva Porto, Soares dos Reis and Henrique Pousão. There is an exhibition of 17th and 18th-century paintings and decorative art in the old dining room and music room of the palace. The new gallery space holds a wide range of temporary exhibitions.
Rua Dom Manuel II. Tel: 22 339 3770. Open: Tue 2–6pm, Wed–Sun 10am–12.30pm & 1.30–6pm. Admission charge. Buses: 3, 20 & 52.

Museu Romântico da Quinta da Macierinha (Romantic Museum of Quinta da Macierinha)

This museum now attempts to recreate a wealthy house in Porto from the 18th century.
Rua de Entre Quintas, 220. Tel: 22 605 7033. Open: Mon–Sat 10am–12.30pm & 2–5.30pm; Sun 2–5.30pm. Bus: 23.

Museu do Carro Eléctrico

Igreja de Santa Clara

Churches and Monasteries

Portugal is a Roman Catholic country with a large number of churches. The styles and periods date from the Middle Ages, reflecting different moods of religious devotion as well as shifts in artistic, cultural and historical representation.

Capela das Almas
This is an 18th-century church that has seen various restorations during the 19th and 20th centuries. Dedicated to St Francis of Assisi and St Catherine, the most distinctive aspects of the chapel are the typical tiles that cover the exterior walls. Inside there is a neo-classical altar, various religious paintings and more tiles.
Rua de Santa Catarina, 428. Buses: 6, 34, 55 & 78.

Igreja da Miseracórdia
Originally built in the 16th century, this church has undergone various changes. It is a significant example of 17th-century architecture in Porto and has an 18th-century frontispiece

Sé Catedral

designed by Nicolas Nasoni, reflecting the rococo influence.
Rua das Flores, 5. Tel: 22 207 4710. Buses: 1, 49 & 93.

Igreja da Ordem do Terço
Built from 1759 by an unknown architect, this church has a carved granite façade with rococo elements. Inside the church you can see stucco and engravings, and the chancel dated 1776 by José Teixeira Guimarães.
Rua de Cimo de Vila. Buses: 20, 21, 22 & 79.

Igreja de Cedofeita
The oldest church in the city, the small Romanesque Igreja de Cedofeita dates back to the 12th century.
Largo do Priorado. Tel: 22 200 5620. Buses: 5, 6 & 34.

Igreja de Nossa Senhora da Esperança
Built between 1724–43 by master António Pereira as the Orphan Girls Asylum. Church construction began 1746, possibly following plans of Nasoni.
Avenida Rodrigues de Freitas. Tel: 22 589 9570. Buses: 35 & 80.

Igreja de Nossa Senhora da Vitória

Built in the 16th century, this classical-style church was renovated in the 18th century. Its focal point is an image of Our Lady, carved in wood by Soares dos Reis.
Rua S Bento da Vitória. Buses: 3, 20 & 52.

Igreja de Santa Clara

The interior of this 15th-century gothic convent is rich in gold carvings. It has undergone changes but the original style remains. Don't miss the Renaissance portico.
Largo 1 de dezembro. Buses: 20, 22 & 23.

Igreja de Santo Ildefonso

This church was rebuilt from ruins in 1737 and covered in *azulejos* in 1932. It has a proto-Baroque polygonal nave, made in wood with stucco ornamentation on the walls and two large rococo-style images.
Largo de Santo Ildefonso. Tel: 22 200 4366. Buses: 22, 23 & 80.

Igreja de São Francisco

A National Monument, this is a Gothic-style convent dating back to the 14th and 15th centuries. The main things to look out for are the church's three naves which were covered in gold during the 17th and 18th centuries, the frescos in the main chapel and the Roman tombs. There is a museum attached to the church with paintings, sculpture, furniture and jewellery on display.
Rua Infante Dom Henrique. Tel: 22 206 2100. Buses: 1, 57 & 91.

Igreja dos Terceiros do Carmo

Constructed in the late 18th century by architect José Figueiredo Seixas, the stonework façade shows influence of Nasoni. The church is crowned by figures of four evangelists.
Rua do Carmo. Tel: 22 207 8400. Buses: 3, 52 & 78.

Igreja dos Carmelitas

Built in the 17th century, the church displays a mixture of classical and Baroque architecture.
Rua do Carmo. Buses: 3, 52 & 78.

Igreja e Torre dos Clérigos

A National Monument and a good place to look over the city, the church and tower were built between 1732–73 by the Clerigos monks, with work by Nicolau Nasoni and master mason António Pereira.
Rua S Felipe de Nery. Tel: 22 200 1729. Buses: 3, 52 & 78.

Sé Catedral

Designated a National Monument, the cathedral was built in Romanesque style in the 12th and 13th centuries. However, various changes took place during the Baroque era (17th and 18th centuries). Nonetheless, the cathedral still has the appearance of a church-fortress with battlements. This was of necessity for it sat on the top of the hill where the first part of the city was built. Look out for the rose window on the main façade, the cloister tiles in the septentrional entry way and the stairway. Inside the cathedral there are various paintings by Nicolau Nasoni. Also worth seeing are the main altar in gilded carving and the altar of the Sacred Sacrament in silver.
Terreiro da Sé. Tel: 22 205 9028. Buses: 3, 6 & 71.

Walk: Churches and Medieval Walls in Ribeira

This walk takes in the city's more important churches and monasteries, which are on a similar route to its medieval walls, the ancient heart of the Ribeira.
Allow 2¹/₂–3 hours.

Start at the Igreja de S Francisco on Rua Infante Dom Henrique.

1 Igreja de São Francisco

This is a Gothic-style convent dating back to the 14th and 15th centuries, although construction on the church itself began in the 12th century. From the outside the church's granite structure is imposing, but when you walk into the church you are struck by the amount of gold leaf. The gold and rococo carvings were only added in the 17th and 18th centuries, turning it into a Baroque masterpiece. However, following the Napoleonic invasions in 1809, the troops used the church as a stable and the décor suffered. It was also bombed during the Civil War of 1828–32. It was finally designated a National Monument in 1984 and today has a small museum alongside with a collection of paintings, sculpture, furniture and catacombs. The old convent was given to the Porto Commercial Association and became the Customs House round the corner.
Open: 9am–5pm (6pm in summer).
Turn left out of the church and along to the Praça do Infante Dom Henrique, going up Rua Mouzinho da Silveira on the northeast side. Take the second right

along Rua da Bainharinha and right up the steep Rua Santana.

The catacombs of Igreja de São Francisco

2 Igreja dos Grillos (São Lourenço)

At the top you will see a Mannerist-style church built by the Jesuits in the 16th and 17th centuries. Take note of the single nave with its panelled semi-circular vault. The symbol of the Jesuits remains on the portal. On the right you can get a good view over the Ribeira. *Tel: 22 200 8056. Open: Tue–Sat 10am–noon & 2–5pm. Bus: 3, 6 & 20. On the left-hand side there are two sets of steps. Take the right ones, which go through to Terreiro da Sé.*

3 Medieval Tower

On the left you will see a medieval tower. In fact, it is not medieval at all but the reconstruction of one found near here when the Cathedral's churchyard was cleared out in the 1940s.

Documents have revealed other tower houses within the primitive enclosure, but they have all disappeared.

4 Sé Catedral

Just past the tower you will see the Romanic Sé Cathedral, which dominates this area. Sitting atop a hill, this was the focal point of the city and everything else was built around it. The original structure was built in the 12th and 13th centuries, and it still retains the style of a church-fortress with battlements, although the cathedral has undergone various changes. The chancel was replaced in Mannerist style in 1610 and the gilt woodcarving is Joanine Baroque from the 18th century.

Look out for the 14th-century statue of Our Lady of Vandoma, Porto's second

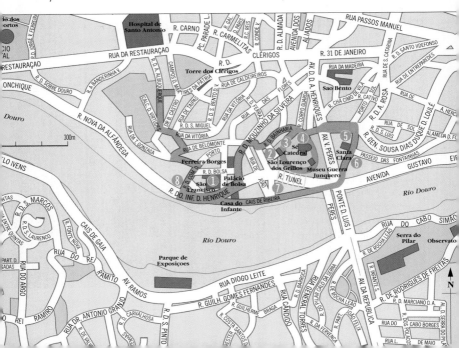

One of the city's most stunning *azulejos* – the cloisters of Sé Catedral

patron saint (the first being Sâo João). It stands on the left of the transept by the Chapel of the Holy Sacrament, which has a silver altar. One of the most stunning features of the cathedral is the Gothic cloister; it is covered in *azulejos* that depict scenes from Solomon's Song of Songs.

Other notable features include the entrance and the stairway designed by Nicolau Nasoni, and the main altar golden carving.

Open: 9am–12.30pm & 2.30–9pm.

The building next door is the Gothic Terreiro da Sé (Bishop's Palace), built in the 13th century and remodelled at the end of the 18th century under the orders of Bishop D Rafael de Mendonça, and also ascribed to Nasoni.

Walk round to the left side of the cathedral, passing the statue of Vimara Peres, and cross the main road to Rua Saraiva Carvalho. On the right you will see a square and archway. Go through the archway.

5 Igreja de Santa Clara

Santa Clara Church, part of a 15th-century gothic convent is rich in gold carvings. It has undergone changes but retained its original style. The Renaissance portico is one of the additions as are the 18th-century carvings and gilt woodwork – the most important examples of the Porto School of Woodcarvers.

Open: 9.30–11.30am & 3–6pm. Bus: 20, 22 & 23. Retrace your steps back to the street, continuing to the right and turn right at Largo do Actor Dias, which leads on to steps downwards.

6 Muralha Fernandina (Guindais Section)

As you walk down you can see the Fernandina Wall on the right. Dating to around 1336–76, it was 3,000 paces long and 9m (30ft) high on average. There were doors in the wall, defended by towers.

Continue down the narrow steps, which take you through a poor residential area. Turn right at the bottom and bear left to the riverfront (don't walk into the tunnel). Continue along here (where there are numerous restaurants) to the Praça da Ribeira.

7 Wall of the Ribeira's Covered Sheds

The main gate used to be located at the Praça da Ribeira. Around the square there were covered sheds. Today only one remains, on the inner façade of the wall.

You can either end your walk here or continue along the riverfront to Rua Nova da Alfândega. On the right you will see steps leading upwards.

8 Muralha Fernandina (Caminho Novo Section)

The steps lead you alongside the most impressive section of the Fernandina Wall, running the length of the stairs of the Caminho Novo. Follow the wall up the steps. At one point it disappears between houses.

Continue up the steps and follow Rua Francisco Rocha to the right, then left and immediately right into Rua A Albuquerque. If you turn right at the top, you find yourself in Campo Mártires da Pátria, close to the Torre dos Clérigos.

In 1996, UNESCO decided that the historic centre of Porto should become a World Heritage Site because its buildings bear testimony to its development in the past millennium or so.

The area defined by UNESCO includes the Sé Cathedral area over to the Igreja de Santa Clara, the Ribeira district down to the river and the Mosteiro da Serra do Pilar on the other side of the river.

The Ribeira in particular had fallen into decline; buildings were dilapidated and it was home to some of the poorer sectors of society. While the authorities are now obliged to protect and renovate the area for the benefit of common heritage, the community is changing. As old residents move to other areas, there is a danger that the community could become fragmented. Meanwhile, the common architectural heritage remains and is slowly being restored to its former glory.

Within the World Heritage Site, there is architecture of distinct periods, from medieval to neo-classical. When a car park was built a few years ago in front of the Palácio da Bolsa, Roman remains were discovered.

Medieval buildings include Sé Cathedral. Situated on a hill, this represents the original site of the city from which everything else radiated outwards. Unsurprising then that other medieval buildings can be found nearby. In the immediate vicinity of the cathedral, a medieval tower was discovered during clearance work in the 1940s. The tower that stands there today is a replica of this. There are also remnants of the original city walls and larger sections of the Muralha Fernandina. Not to be missed is the Casa do Infante, the supposed birthplace of Henry the Navigator.

As with many churches, the Sé consists of renovations and reconstructions from various architectural periods. Baroque elements can be seen here, particularly in the sacristy and cloisters. The most renowned architects from this period

Above: Plaque relating the history of the ancient Muralha Fernandina
Facing page: Porto's neo-classical Custom House

were António Pereira and Nicolau Nasoni, whose most famous works in this area include the Torre dos Clérigos, the façade of the Igreja da Misericórdia and the Palácio de São João. The most splendid examples of Porto's Baroque architecture are in the Igreja de São Francisco and the Igreja de Santa Clara, with elaborate woodcarvings and gold leaf work.

During the 18th and 19th centuries, Porto underwent a period of renovation, much of which was organised by João de Almada. Neo-classical architecture demonstrates the influence of the English in the city at this time,

particularly the Feitoria Inglesa (linked to the consul John Whitehead) and the Hospital de Santo António (designed by John Carr). However, Porto architect Carlos Amarante also left his mark with the construction of the Igreja da Ordem Terceira da Trindade. Other neo-classical buildings include the Palácio da Bolsa and the Edifício da Alfândega.

The appearance of impressive *azulejos* are also prevalent, both within the heritage area and beyond. Good examples can be seen in the cloisters of Sé Cathedral, Igreja de Santa Clara, Igreja de Santo Ildefonso, Igreja do Carmo and the Estação de São Bento.

Walk: Porto's Architectural Styles

This walk takes in a few examples of Porto's architectural styles, from medieval to neo-classical, starting in the Ribeira and ending in the shopping district of the Old Town.

Allow 2–3 hours. Start in Rua da Alfândega.

1 Casa do Infante

At No 47 you will find the Casa do Infante, built in the early 14th century as both a customs house and a residence for royal officials.

At the end of the 16th century, the mint attached to it. Although there were major alterations in the 17th century, it remained a customs house until the 19th century. Its biggest claim to fame is that the Infante D Henrique, Prince Henry the Navigator, was born here. Today you can visit the house and museum.

Rua da Alfândega, 10. Tel: 22 200 1987. Open: Mon–Fri 8.30am–5pm. Turn right out of the house and take the first left along Rua do Infante Dom Henrique. This brings you to a square of the same name.

2 Palácio da Bolsa Stock Exchange

On the west side of the square, on Rua Ferreira Borges, you will see the Stock Exchange building. A neo-classical building, construction started in 1842. It is worth paying the small fee to go inside. Highlights include the Pátio das Nações, the granite and marble staircase, and the highly decorated rooms covered in paintings; is particularly special.

Rua de Ferreira Borges. Tel: 22 339 9000. Walk up Ferreira Borges. On the left you will see the Instituto do Vinho do Porto and on the right the old Mercado Ferreira Borges.

3 Mercado Ferreira Borges

Completed in 1888, this old market building is an example of Porto's architectural ironwork. It functioned as a fruit market between 1939 and 1978 and now presents cultural events.

Continue past the market, turning right and immediately left up Rua das Flores.

4 Igreja da Miseracórdia

On the left you will see the Miseracórdia Church. Built in the second half of the 16th century, the frontispiece was rebuilt by Nicolau Nasoni in the 18th century and demonstrates rococo influence.

Open: Mon–Sat 9am–noon & 2–6pm. Take the first left after the church and immediately right, continuing to the top of a steep little road. On the left you will see the Centro Português de Fotografia (CPF), installed in 2001 after the old Cadeia da Relação prison was remodelled. Turn right and walk down to the Clérigos Tower.

5 Igreja e Torre dos Clérigos (Clerigos Church and Tower)

Built by Nasoni in the 18th century, this Baroque tower and church is now a National Monument and a city landmark. The interior of the church has detailed Baroque-rococo decoration and the tower stands 75.6m (248ft) high. You can go to the top, but it is not recommended for small children as there are too many nooks and crannies to fall down. From the top, there is a great view over the city.

You can stop here or turn back towards the CPF. On the right is a green square, the Campo Mártires da Pátria. Walk along the right-hand side of this, past the anonymous white statue. On the other side, cross over to Rua da Restauração and take the first right up Rua Alberto Gomes. Turn left down Rua de Dom Manuel II.

6 Museu Nacional Soares dos Reis

This 18th-century neo-classical Palace was built on the order of the Mendes de Morais and Castro brothers. Later it became a silver braid factory, but it was bought by the royal family who gave it away to the Miseracordia religious order in 1862. It became a museum in 1937.

The neoclassical façade of the Museu Nacional Soares dos Reis

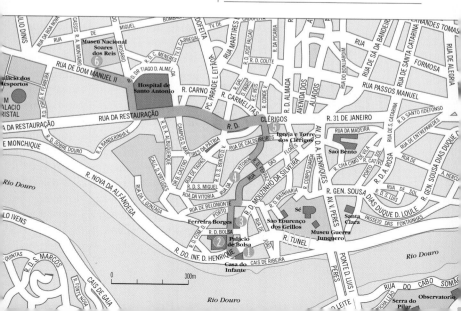

No visitor to Portugal can fail to notice the prevalence of *azulejos* (hand-painted ceramic tiles) – from small panels to large-scale frescos they can be seen on the walls of churches, palaces, houses and other secular buildings, and there is the more modern phenomenon of decorating the metro stations. More than a utilitarian or decorative addition to a room or a building, they reflect the artistic, cultural, political and economic trends of the country, its traditions and innovations and, in short, its history.

The first known tiles in Portugal were of Arab origin, imported from factories in Seville in the early 16th century until Portuguese production started a few years later. Due to the Moorish occupation of the Iberian peninsular for seven centuries, the tiles became a permanent element, as did the old methods of production.

While the Moorish tiles were covered in geometric patterns, the Portuguese

started to introduce their own themes – European vegetation and animals were particularly popular during the Gothic and Renaissance periods. The use of Italian majolica ceramic techniques meant that tiles could be painted directly, allowing for more detailed decoration and colour. Often, though, large spaces like churches and palaces opted for tiles with repetitive patterns.

During the 17th century, the styles became more elaborate, with pictorial representations produced in panels and covering entire walls or spaces. As well as themes from Ancient Rome, painters produced 'exotic' images (brought back by the explorers) mixed with religious symbols. Every kind of space could be decorated in tiles, both civil and sacred.

Around the end of the 17th century, large-scale figurative panels were produced in Holland, becoming very popular with the Portuguese. The superior quality of the Dutch techniques led to training in Portugal and thus the reduction in imports. By the 18th century, tile painters were masters in

their art. With more scope for creativity, scenes were designed according to the architectural space. Tile factories sprung up and a great period of production emerged, coinciding with the reign of Dom João V (1706–50).

Influences during the 18th century included the French Regency styles, particularly the rococo, and *pombaline,* the functional style encouraged by the Marquês de Pombal during the reconstruction that followed the Lisbon Great Earthquake of 1755. During the neo-classic era, panels were decorated with frescos, often narrating social scenes and featuring elegant figures of the era.

The economic slump that accompanied the French invasions (1807–11) in the early 19th century meant that functional cheap semi-industrial tiles were used to cover buildings. Master painters found

work elsewhere and anything beyond the simple repetitive tile was a crude imitation of the previous artistic frescos. However, the Romantic period saw a resurgence of elaborate scenes and production, with exuberant panels of flowers, trees and allegorical figures.

By the 20th century, styles had become more eclectic, with colours and styles following the Modernist and Art Deco art movements. The 1950s saw the return of the functional with the decoration of Lisbon's metro stations, but now the functional was mixed with Abstract art styles that fully involved the viewer. This has continued to the present day with artists decorating new buildings and underground stations, still developing and experimenting with their techniques, styles and colour.

For examples of some of the best *azulejos* in Porto, see the following walk (*pp116–117*). In Lisbon you should see the Museu Nacional do Azulejo (*see p30*), which covers the history and different styles of the tiles from inception until the present day. Other prime examples close to Lisbon include: the Palácio Benfica; the Capela de São Filipe in the castle in Setúbal and the Palácio Nacional de Sintra.

Facing page above: São Bento Station displays amazing *azulejos* (tiled panels)
Facing page below: 18th-century *azulejos* in the Museu Nacional do Azulejo
This page: 20th-century *azulejos* in the Museu Nacional do Azulejo

Walk: *Azulejos* in the Old Town

Although there are examples of *azulejos* around every corner, this walk guides you round some of the best in the city, passing through the central shopping district of the old town, past the historic viewing point at Clerigos Tower and ending at Carmo Church by the university. More tiles can be seen on the church walk on pp106–7.

Allow 1–1 1/2 hours

Start on Rua de Santa Catarina on the corner with Rua de Fernandes Tomás.

1 Capela das Almas

On the corner you will see a chapel covered in the distinctive Portuguese tiles. Dating back to the 18th century, the chapel was renovated at the beginning of the 19th century, but it was not until 1929 that the exterior walls were entirely re-covered in tiles. The images here represent scenes from the lives of St Francis of Assisi and St Catherine, to whom the chapel pays homage.

There are more *azulejos* inside the nave of the church. Until renovations have finished the tiles are protected by a thin layer of gauze, but you can still see them.

Turning left out of the church, walk down Rua de Santa Catarina, maybe stopping off at the splendid Café Majestic on the left just before Rua Passos Manuel or doing a little window shopping. Cross over this street, going up hill to Largo de Santo Ildefonso.

Tiles can be seen all over the city

2 Igreja de Santo Ildefonso

On the left-hand side by the recently renovated small square, you will see the Santo Ildefonso church, covered in tiles by Jorge Colaço. They depict scenes from the life of the saint and allegories of the Eucharist. Although these only date from 1932, the church is much older than this. It was reconstructed in the first half of the 18th century, after falling into ruin.

Turn right out of the church and walk left down Rua 31 de Janeiro. Turn left into Praça de Almeida Garrett.

3 Estação São Bento

On the left you will see São Bento
Station. Built at the beginning of the
20th century on the grounds of a
convent with the same name, the
entrance hall contains one of the most
spectacular examples of *azulejos* from
that period. The work of painter Jorge
Colaço (1864–1942), the 20,000 tiles
depict images of railway history and
celebrated moments in Portuguese
history.

*Turn right out of the station, crossing
over and turning left up Avenida dos
Aliados. Walk up towards Clerigos Tower
(see p113), turning right on to
Carmelitas and continuing to Praca
Gomes.*

4 Igreja do Carmo

On the far side of this little square,
leading into Praça Carlos Alberto, you
will see Carmo Church next to Igreja
dos Carmelitas, which is also worth a
visit. The right wall of Carmo is covered
in *azulejos*. Designed by Silvester
Silvestro in 1912, the tiles pay homage
to Our Lady and form the largest
ceramic panel in the city.

*From here you can continue back down-
town, downhill to the Ribeira or onto the
Museu Nacional Soares dos Reis and the
Palácio de Cristal. You're close to the
university here so there are also various
cafés and places to have a light lunch.*

Open: Mon–Fri 7.30am–noon & 2–5pm,
Sat 8am–noon & Sun 7.30am–1.15pm.

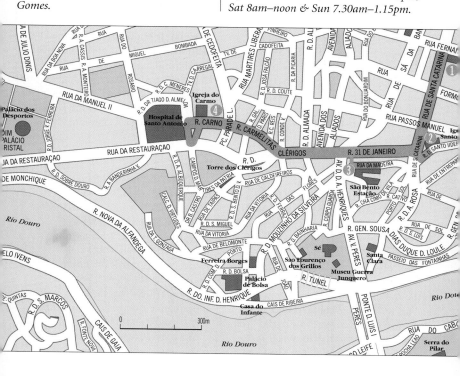

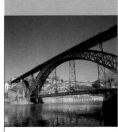

Ponte D Luis I

Porto's Bridges

Ever since Roman times, there has been a need to cross the River Douro from Porto to Vila Nova de Gaia. However, the first bridge only appeared in 1806, close to the Ribeira. Until then traders and travellers crossed by boat.

Built to facilitate travel and communication from the north to the south of the country, the **Ponte das Barcas** was constructed in wood. When French Napoleonic troops entered the city in 1807, a large proportion of the population fled across the bridge. Unable to hold the weight, the bridge collapsed, killing hundreds. The bridge was reconstructed but set alight by the French as they fled from English and Portuguese troops led by the Duke of Wellington. Luckily, the citizens of Gaia got enough wood together in a short time to get them across the river. The life of the bridge finally came to an end when the **Ponte Pênsil** was built in 1843.

Designed by the engineers Mellet and Bigot, the Ponte Pênsil was the first permanent bridge across the river. Officially, it was called the Ponte Dona Maria II yet it was never known by that name, but by a nickname that related to its structure (pensile or suspended). Taken out of action in 1887, two of the stone obelisks that stood at either end of the bridge remain on the north side of the river, next to the **Ponte Dom Luís I**.

In 1876, the **Ponte Maria Pia** was constructed as a railway bridge to take passengers from Vila Nova de Gaia to Porto's Campanhã Station. The first major work by Gustave Eiffel, the bridge remained in service until the **Ponte São João** was constructed alongside it in 1991. Built by controversial civil engineer Edgar Cardoso, this bridge has a trestle-style structure with three spans supported by two pillars that stand deep in the Douro riverbed.

The bridge that is most familiar to the tourists in images that promote the city is the **Ponte Dom Luis I**. Designed by an assistant of Gustave Eiffel, it was opened in 1886 and has two levels open to traffic and pedestrians. The highest one, which stands at 172m (564ft) high and offers fantastic views over the Douro and the two cities, will eventually be closed to road traffic because the metro will run across it.

Further downriver lies the **Ponte Arrábida**, the largest concrete bridge in the world when it opened in 1963. Also built by Cardoso, the bridge has a 270m span and when it was inaugurated it won acclaim from internationally renowned civil engineers. Upriver is the **Ponte do Freixo**, opened in 1995. Both are highway bridges that facilitate movement around and through the city as traffic and travel increase.

Since the advent of the industrial revolution, bridges have been an important part of the development of Porto. In 2001, when the city celebrated its status as European City of Culture, it chose 'Bridges to the Future' as its theme and designed a bridge logo. The decision was made to build another bridge to provide a replacement to the upper level of Dom Luís I when the metro is up and running. The **Ponte Infante Henrique**, between Dom Luis and Pia Maria, thus links the city's most famous son, Henry the Navigator, with its future.

The more modern Ponte da Arrábida

Walk: Ponte Dom Luis I to Vila Nova de Gaia

This walk takes you from Porto to Vila Nova de Gaia, the city just across the river, with fantastic views of both. At the end of the walk you can visit one (or more) Port wine houses.

Allow 3–4 hours.

Start outside São Bento Station. Walk left down Avenida Dom Afonso Henriques, which leads into Avenida Vimara Peres. On the right-hand side there is a road running parallel to this which keeps you away from the main road. Go up this and turn back on to the main road at the Sé Cathedral and along the path across the bridge.

1 Ponte Dom Luís I

The upper level of this bridge (*see pp118–19*) is 172m (564ft) high, so if you prefer you can start from the Ribeira and walk across the lower level. However, you do get fantastic views from up here. As you walk south, you can see the Fernandina Wall on the left, and on the right the signs of the Port wine caves in Vila Nova de Gaia, with the *rabelo* boats and the Ponte de Arrábida in the distance. Upriver are four bridges. *Once you reach the other side of the bridge, there is a small road leading to the right. Here there is a viewing point across to the Ribeira. Follow the road round to the left. Cross over the main road. Go up the ramp on the left.*

2 Mosteiro da Serra do Pilar

This leads to the Mosteiro da Serra do Pilar with its curious 16th-century circular church. Most of it is off limits because it belongs to the army, but you can visit the church. Look out for its hemispheric vault and narrow balcony. Inside you can see 18th-century carved images, and the unique circular cloister. It was classified as a World Heritage Monument by UNESCO in 1996. There are more good views of Porto from here. *Come back down the ramp and turn right towards the bridge, but take the right turning down the cobbled street on the right. Follow this road steeply downhill. It bends round to the left and eventually comes out on the lower level of the bridge.*

3 Vila Nova de Gaia

As well as a good view of the Ribeira across the river, this is the place to take a cruise along the River Douro and, of course, to visit the Port wine caves. Only 16 of the Port wine companies offer visits, although there are many more. The map shows the ones that offer guided tours and tastings. *To get back from Vila Nova de Gaia you can either take a bus from the riverfront towards the Ponte Dom Luís I, or walk back across the lower level and left into the Ribeira.*

Port Wine Houses with Guided Tours

A **A A Calém & Filho, SA**, *Avenida Diogo Leite, 26*; **Calém Ponte**, *Largo da Ponte D Luîs I.*

B **A A Ferreira, SA**, *Rua da Carvalhosa, 19/103.*

C **Barros**, *Rua Dom Leonor de Freitas, 182.*

D **Cockburn/Martinez**, *Rua Dom Leonor de Freitas.*

E **Croft**, *Largo Joaquim Magalhães, 23.*

F **J W Burmester & Ca, SA**, *Travessa Barão Forrester, 56.*

G **Kopke**, *Rua Serpa Pinto, 183.*

H **Offley Forrester**, *Rua de Choupelo, 62.*

I **Osborne**, *Rua Cândido dos Reis, 670.*

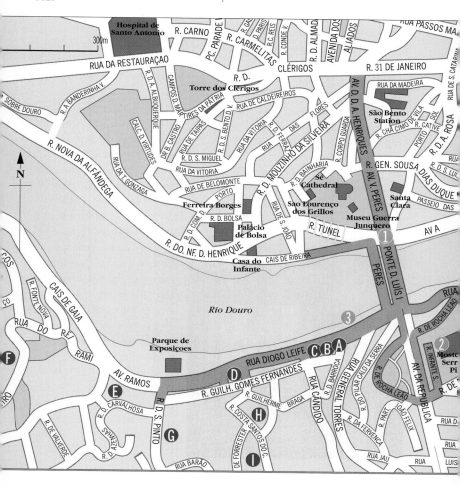

Port Wine

Porto is famed for its fortified wine – those that know little or nothing about the city will probably have sampled or seen Port wine. During the near two millennia that it has been produced, Port has become a cultural symbol at the very heart of the people, and a key national export.

The grapes are cultivated in the green valleys of the River Douro, and the wine warehouses are located in the city of Vila Nova de Gaia, on the south bank of the river, just across the bridge from Porto.

Although cultivation and production of wine can be traced back to the 3rd century, the actual designation of Port wine only dates from the 17th century. The number of British wine merchants was on the increase and exports were rising. There were also Dutch and German merchants, but the 1703 Treaty of Methuen meant a trade exchange with the British – they favoured Portuguese wine for the import of British textiles.

Following rivalries and fraud amongst producers in the 18th century and the slump in exports due to complaints of bad produce, the Marquês de Pombal created the Companhia Geral dos Vinhos do Alto Douro in 1756 to ensure the future quality of the product. He also created the first demarcated wine area in the Douro valley to indicate the fine wine area.

After battling against the phyloxera pest and cheap imitations from overseas in the 19th century, the Port wine industry has seen various regulations in the production, sale and export of the product since 1907, along with changes in the demarcation areas. Port wine lodges appeared in Vila Nova de Gaia when the Entreposto was created in 1926 – a new demarcation area that obliged all producers who wanted to age their wine to have a lodge there.

Various organisations have been set up over the years to regulate and oversee the production and quality of Port, including the Instituto do Vinho do Porto (Port Wine Institute), the Association of Port Wine Companies and the Interprofessional Commission for the Demarcated Region of the Douro.

Types of Port Wine

There are various different types of Port wine, named according to the blending, quality and ageing process, and made from 90 different types of grape. After a time in the barrel, the wine is fortified by adding brandy.

Ruby is made with a blend of grapes from several harvests, and spends two or three years in the barrel before bottling.

Tawny wines are also made from a blend of grapes and spend at least six years in the barrel before being fortified and bottled. In the process they become more brown than red.

Aged Tawny are blended wines that spend a longer period in the barrel, from 10–40 years.

Colheita is made from a single blend, but in a similar way to tawny and is bottled after seven years. It should ideally be consumed a year after bottling.

White Port is made from white grapes and ranges in colour from pale yellow to a golden white, depending on the sweetness or dryness.

Late Bottled Vintage (LBV) wines are made with good grapes from a single harvest, but not good enough to be vintage. The wine is held in the barrel at least six years and filtered before bottling.

Vintage wines are produced with the best grapes from each harvest and bottled after two or three years. They are the only wines that age in the bottle (15–50 years). Therefore, once they are opened, they must be decanted and drunk quickly (48 hours) before the air ruins the flavour.

RABELO BOATS

These flat-bottomed boats were the traditional way of transporting the barrels from the Douro to the wine lodge for bottling. This form of transport ended in 1964, but during the festivities for São João in June, a *rabelo* boat race is held to bring them back to life. You can also see a few of them alongside the quay in Vila Nova de Gaia, advertising the lodge to which they belong.

Facing page: Port wine houses line the riverside
Above: Port comes in various blends, ages and prices

Fundação Serralves (Serralves Foundation)

The Serralves Foundation was founded in 1989 as a partnership between the government and various entities and private organisations. It bought the pink Casa de Serralves and gardens, and opened the modern new building of the Museu de Arte Contemporânea in 1999.

Modern sculpture in the Serralves gardens

Casa de Serralves

The pink, 1930s Casa de Serralves is both a museum and the headquarters of the foundation. Originally intended as a house, the Casa is a unique example of Art Deco work, built on the orders of the second Conde de Vizela Alberto Cabral. The project was finally finished by Portuguese architect Marqûes da Silva in 1940, and was initially intended as a luxurious private residence. In 1996 the building was declared to be of 'public interest'.

Serralves Parque

The park is a living example of *paisagismo* (landscape painting) of the 20th-century Impressionists. Strongly influenced by the French school, the park was finished in 1940 following the project of Jacques Gréber.

There are various sections to the park, each with its own characteristics. At the back of the house is a formal garden surrounded by walls and trees with stepping stones that lead you to a little lake called Lago Romântico. Beyond here, the garden leads towards the fields and herb garden to the end of the park where the old stables and other rural constructions are located.

Going back towards the house, to the north are the recently created gardens of the Museu de Arte Contemporânea, designed to blend in with the developing surroundings and the building, as well as allowing for outdoor exhibitions. Further on is the rose garden, the Jardim do Relógio de Sol and the gardens of the Casa. The rose garden is one of the best in the country.

Museu de Arte Contemporânea

Porto's foremost modern art museum located in the Serralves Foundation's grounds just off Boavista, the Museu de Arte Contemporânea was designed by internationally renowned Portuguese architect Alvaro Siza (*see pp74–5*). Opened in 1999, the design of the building allows ultimate flexibility of space, which is needed for the exhibitions on show here. Of the 12,700m^2 (136,652 sq ft), more than a third is for exhibitions. The outside of the building is painted granite and plaster, with smooth lines and sharp corners.

The exhibition area is divided into various rooms, each on a different scale. The rooms vary in light and are united by a large U-shaped gallery that occupies most of the ground floor area. The majority of the exhibitions feature art created after 1960.

There is a permanent collection of art dating from 1960 to the present. The 1960s were a time of political agitation that affected everyone. Moreover, Pop Art, Minimalism, Conceptualism and 'Land Art' emerged at this time. The museum's permanent collection represents the most important contributions of artists from this era.

Some of the international artists included in the permanent collection include Georg Baselitz, Hans-Peter Feldman, Hamish Fulton, Dan Graham, Blinky Palermo, Ed Ruscha and Gilberto Zorio, and Portuguese artists include Alberto Carneiro, Julião Sarmento, Ângelo de Sousa and Ana Vieira, amongst others.

The museum also has a high-tech, 260-seat auditorium, a library and documentation centre, a café and restaurant, and a terrace with a view over the park. The auditorium has a variety of functions, presenting concerts, films and theatre, dance and small conferences.

The Art Deco style of the Casa de Serralves

Walk: Serralves to Palácio de Cristal

This walk is quite long, but you can always hop on a bus to take you to the next feature or drop out at any time. You will see various aspects of Porto life, from the modern architectural designs of Serralves and the Casa da Música to the Museu Romântico, passing upmarket residential properties, the financial district and three different gardens.

Allow 3–4 hours.

Start outside the gate of the Fundação Serralves in Avenida do Marechal Gomes da Costa. You can get the No 35 bus to Rua de Dom Francisco Almeida just round the corner.

1 Fundação Serralves
At the entrance to the Museu de Arte Contemporânea, you can buy a ticket for both the garden and the museum. As well as numerous interesting exhibitions, the structure of the museum is a must-see for those that appreciate modern architecture. Everything here was designed by Alvaro Siza, from the

The gardens of the Serralves Foundation

PORTO – CITY OF CULTURE

In 2001, Porto was European City of Culture with the Dutch city of Rotterdam. This brought a wealth of performances by internationally renowned musicians, dancers and artists, and involved the community. The status also led to the renovation of numerous parks and buildings with the remodelling of the old Cadeia (prison) in the city centre, which became the Centro Português de Fotografia. A new musical cultural centre was proposed with high-tech studios, a philharmonic orchestra and choir and educational programmes for children. However, although the Casa da Música is still under construction, many of the musical projects take place elsewhere.

outside to the inside, even the chairs of the restaurant. Knowing this, you can appreciate how everything comes together harmoniously into a unified form. The meals are good here; when you have exhausted yourself inside the museum, have a decent lunch and walk it off in the beautiful and therapeutic quietness of the gardens.

As you step into the first part of the garden, you are likely to see some outdoor art. The pathway leads to the Casa de Serralves, the pink Art Deco building where you can have a cup of tea and enjoy the modern masterpieces that occasionally exhibit here. The back of the house looks over the formal gardens and, from here, you can wander

past the pond to the end of the property. Stay as long as you like, but you may be reluctant to leave.

Rua D João de Castro, 210. Tel: 22 615 6500. Open: Nov–Mar Tue–Sun 10am–7pm (Thur until 10pm; Apr–Oct Tue–Sun 10am–8pm (Thur until 10pm). Either return to the entrance you started at and turn right out of the gate and right down Rua de Serralves, or get on bus No 35 and ask for the Jardim Botânico in Campo Alegre. Or, if it is open, you can exit from the front of the Casa de Serralves into this street, turn right and continue to the bottom. Don't take the left fork, but continue to the end of the road, which bends round and brings you out on to Rua do Campo Alegre by the Ipanema

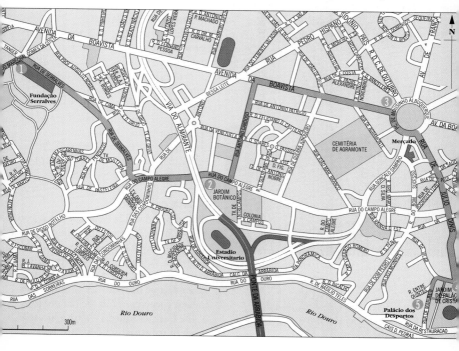

Classical sculpture in the Jardim do Palácio de Cristal

Park Hotel. Turn left here, pass the Centro Comercial Campo Alegre and go under the bridge.

2 Jardim Botânico do Porto (Porto's Botanical Gardens)

On the right-hand side you will see the entrance to the botanical gardens, which are set in the grounds of the Faculty of Science of the University of Porto. This is itself located in an old palace, built by Brazilian João Silva Monteiro in 1875 on the grounds of an old mansion house. The garden was planted when João Henrique Andresen Júnior purchased the property in 1895. The state then bought the property and decreed the garden as botanical in 1951, administered by the Faculty of Sciences. Today the garden consists of a historical section divided into three parts: lakes with aquatic plants, flowerbeds and greenhouses. The gardens have recently been overhauled and reopened to the public.

Open: Oct–Mar, 9am–6pm & Apr–Sept, 10am–5pm. Come out of the gardens and go down Rua António Cardoso opposite (or take bus No 35 and get off outside the Palácio de Cristal in Rua de Manuel II). If you are walking, notice the Galeria Cordoeira on the right-hand side and the headquarters and grounds (which you can visit) of the Centro Português de Fotografia on the left. At the end of the street turn right on to Boavista.

3 Casa da Música

Walk down Avenida Boavista where you will see modern residential buildings alongside shopping complexes, and old mansions sandwiched in between. You will come to the Praça de Mousinho de Albuquerque in about ten minutes. On the left corner you can see the progress of the Casa da Música – a complicated modern construction designed by architect Souto Moura as the emblem of Porto 2001. The building will probably not be finished until late 2003 or early 2004. When completed, it will be a high-tech cultural centre, focusing particularly on music.

Take the third right down Rua de Julio Dinis, passing through a shopping and financial area. At the end of the street, turn right on to Rua de Manuel II and cross to the other side.

4 Jardim do Palácio de Cristal

Planted in the 19th century, these lush gardens were designed by architect Emile David and offer fabulous views over the River Douro. There is also a multifunction pavilion here, built in 1956 to replace the former Crystal Palace, which was built for the International Exhibition in 1865. The current building has a restaurant and café, and holds exhibitions. For Porto 2001, the Almeida Garrett Library was constructed to one side of the park. *Head to the west side of the park and you will find a gate leading down to the Museu Romântico.*

The door on the right is the entrance to the museum. Here Carlos Alberto, the exiled king of Sardinia spent his last days before he died in 1843. You can see the museum's collection of decorative art from the period. Back outside, the left-hand door is the entrance to the final and well-deserved stop, the Solar do Vinho do Porto.

5 Solar do Vinho de Porto

If you are too tired to visit the Romantic Museum, end this long walk by sampling some Port wine at the Solar do Vinho do Porto via the neighbouring entrance of the same building. The Solar is located in the 19th-century Quinta da Macierinha manor house where King Carlos Alberto of Sardinia died in 1849. Today the building houses the Romantic Museum and the Solar on the ground floor. Relax in luxury armchairs with a few glasses of Port, and views over the Douro.

If it is late by the time you emerge from the Solar, you will not be able to go back through the gardens. Go out of the main gate and to the right and turn right at the top, back on to Rua de Manuel II.

A more modern artistic touch in the Jardim do Palácio de Cristal

Excursions from Porto

Amarante

Amarante is a beautiful place to take a day trip. You can visit the 16th-century **Mosteiro de São Gonçalo**, founded by Dom João III and Dona Catarina. It has a museum-library, two cloisters, and a church with a mixture of Renaissance and Baroque architecture. The **São Gonçalo Bridge**, just a few metres away, was originally a medieval bridge over the Rio Tâmega, but the three arches there now were constructed in the 18th century. Also worth seeing are the **Igreja de Santo Domingo** and **Igreja de São Pedro**.

Amarante is located 63km (39 miles) from Porto along the A4-IP4 towards Vila Real. Monastery is found in Praça da República. Open: daily 8am–6pm. Train: Porto to Amarante, change in Livração, takes approximately 2 hours.

Aveiro

Aveiro has a variety of things to see and is known for its Ria (lagoon with tides) and its canals, along which *moliceiros* (flat-bottomed boats) travel to the centre of the town. While there you should visit the **Catedral** with its Baroque façade, carved and gilded interior and 18th-century paintings. In addition to various other churches, there are a number of houses around the city centre in Art Nouveau style, especially around the Central Canal.

Amarante is 67km (42 miles) south of Porto along the A1-IP1. Trains: leave several times each hour from Porto's Campanhã station and take 1 hour.

Barcelos

Located on the River Cávado, Barcelos is renowned for its ceramics and other craft markets, and the cockerel that is emblematic of Portugal. The Feira de Barcelos market takes place every week on the Campo da República.

Located about 50km (31 miles) north of Porto, just off the A3-IP1 towards Braga.

Braga

Braga is the centre of the textile industry in Portugal, located 53km

You can drift downriver in a hired boat at the beautiful town of Amarante

(33 miles) northeast of Porto. It was founded by the Celts in 300 BC and later occupied by the Romans. The city has an historic centre with several monuments not to be missed, including the medieval **Sé Catedral** and the 16th-century Italian Renaissance **Igreja da Misericórdia**. There are also numerous museums such as the **Museu de Arte**

Sacra, the **Museu de D Diogo de Sousa** and the **Museu dos Biscaínhos**.
Braga is located 53km (33 miles) from Porto along the A3-IP1.

Sé Catedral
Although the cathedral was originally medieval and considered the oldest in Portugal, it has been renovated and

reconstructed over the years, leaving a patchwork of styles from different periods. The Romanesque structure is still evident, but there is also a Gothic-Flemish tomb holding the Infante Afonso, a *Manuelino* baptismal font, Baroque-style organs, and 14th-century carved frescos and choir stalls.
Rossio da Sé. Open: daily 8.30am–1pm & 2–6.30pm.

Bom Jesus do Monte

This monument, just outside Braga, is famous for its numerous steps leading up to the church. Dating back to the 15th century, it was built under the orders of the Archbishop Dom Jorge da Costa. Since then several parts have been reconstructed, but the alterations in 1723 were the most significant, giving it much the look it has today.

There is an elevator inside the monument which works on water pressure. Open since 1882, it is the oldest elevator of its kind still functioning.
Located 5km (3 miles) from Braga along the N103. Open: Sun–Fri.

Coimbra

Quite a journey south of Porto (117km, 73 miles), Coimbra is best visited on your way to Lisbon (197km, 122.5 miles further south) or for a weekend trip. Dating back to pre-Roman times when it was a fortified settlement, Coimbra became the first capital of the country before Lisbon. It also boasts the country's oldest university.

You can see pre-Roman ruins at **Porta de Almedina** (Almedina Gate), which itself dates back to the 9th century. Look

The Santuário do Bom Jesus do Monte near Braga deserves a visit

out for the 13th-century **Torre da Estrela**, the vaulted ceiling of the 12th-century cathedral **Sé Velha**; the first Gothic cloister in the country; the

QUEIMA DAS FITAS

A good time to visit Coimbra is in May, when the Queima das Fitas (Burning of the Academic Ribbons) takes place. This is a student festival that marks the beginning of a month of revision before the June exams. The festival week features serenades, suppers, a ball, bullfights, parades and the ceremonial ribbon burning.

Claustro de Celas; the **Velha Universidade** (Old University) and the **Repúblicas,** the 14th-century student accommodation buildings. There are several museums in the city, including the **Museu Nacional Machado de Castro,** which has an impressive collection of 16th-century Flemish and 15th–16th-century Portuguese paintings, and ceramics, sculptures and jewellery.

Coimbra is located 117km (73 miles) south from Porto along the A3-IP1. Cathedral: Largo da Sé Velha. Open: daily 9.30am–12.30pm & 2–5.30pm.

Statue of D Afonso Henriques in Guimarães, where the nation was born

Museu Nacional Machado de Castro: Rúa de São João. Open: Tue–Sun 9.30am–12.30pm & 2–5pm. Velha Universidade: Patio das Escolas. Open: daily 9.30am–noon & 2–5pm. Trains: leave every hour and take around 40 minutes.

Guimarães

Guimarães is known as the birthplace of the Portuguese nation and today is a National Heritage Site because its first king, Dom Afonso Henrique, was born here and set off from here on the reconquest against the Moors. There are so many historic monuments in the centre that you really need more than a day, but the must-sees include the **Castelo de São Miguel,** the **Igreja de Nossa Senhora da Oliveira** and the **Convento e Igreja de Santo Domingo.** The **Briteiros pre-Roman settlement** close by is also worth a visit.

Located 42km (26 miles) northeast from Porto just off the A3-IP1 from Porto to Braga.

Castelo de São Miguel

As well as the medieval castle and walls, there is a chapel inside. Austere and Romanesque, the chapel contains tombs of noble warriors who fought for the foundation of the nation.

Rua Conde Dom Henrique. Open: daily 9am–6.30pm (5.30pm in winter).

Citânia de Briteiros

Just 15km (8 miles) from Guimarães, lie the ruins of an important pre-Roman settlement, once a town encircled by three walls. The ruins have undergone extensive study and there is evidence of

Castle at Santa Maria de Feira

Roman influence here. Today it is a
UNESCO World Heritage Site, protected
as part of the common cultural heritage.
*Located 15km (9 miles) north of
Guimarães along the N101. Open: daily
May–Sept, 9am–7.30pm, Oct–Apr,
9am–6pm.*

Lamego

Situated in the Douro's wine producing
area, there are also several interesting
churches here. In particular, the
**Santuário de Nossa Senhora dos
Remedios** (*Monte de Santo Estêvão;
open: daily*), a pilgrimage site that
celebrates a festival with a procession
and games every August. Also, see the
Museu de Lamego (*Largo Luis de
Camões; open Tue–Sat 10am–12.30pm*

*& 2–5pm, Sun & public holidays
10am–12.30pm*), found in the old **Paço
Episcopal** (Episcopal Palace), with a
collection of Portuguese paintings from
the 16th–18th centuries, old cars and
azulejos.
*Located about 80km (50 miles) from
Porto along the A4-IP4 to Vila Real, then
the IP3 south to Lamego. Santuário:
Monte de Santo Estêvão. Museu de
Lamego: Largo de Camões.
Open: Tue–Sun.*

Santa Maria de Feira

The village of Santa Maria de Feira
has one of the prettiest castles in the
country. It originated as early as the
10th century, but building continued,
and the original barely remains.

Nevertheless, it is a fantasy castle that dominates the skyline of the town. You should also see the 17th-century *azulejos* (tiles) at the **Convento dos Loios**. The town itself was named after the fairs that have taken place since the 12th century. Today there is a market every month. *Located 25km (15.5 miles) south of Porto along the A1-IP1. Castle: Largo do Castelo. Open: Tue–Sun.*

Vila do Conde

This quiet fishing village was once a centre of shipbuilding. Located on the River Lima, it retains its historic centre, which includes the 14th-century

Mosteiro de Santa Clara (you can only visit the church and cloisters), part of the aqueduct, and the 16th-century **Igreja Matriz** (*Rua da Igreja; tel: 25 263 1327; open: daily 8.30am–noon & 4–8pm*), which has a *Manuelino* portico. The **Escola de Rendas** (*Rua de São Bento; tel: 25 224 8470; open: Tue–Thur 9.30am–noon & 2–5pm, Fri 9.30am–noon*) is the lace-making school, for which the village is famous. *Located 20km (12.5 miles) north of Porto along the coastal road towards Viana do Castelo. Mosteiro: Largo Dom Afonso Sanches. Church open daily 9am–noon & 2–5.30pm.*

Aqueduct at Vila do Conde

Getting Away from it All

As well as the historic sites, wine caves and cultural institutions in Porto's city centre, there are plenty of places to escape nearby. These range from the beauty of the Douro Valley and the beaches of Espinho and Matoshinhos to the city parks and wine tours.

Beach at Espinho

Boat Trips along the Douro

Boat trips on the River Douro are a relaxing way to see part of the city and to take in the sights of the Douro Valley further upstream. They come in various packages: you can take quick city trips, lasting less than an hour; cruises with lunch or dinner; all-day trips upstream with lunch and port, and stops at interesting villages with a train trip back; and longer cruises of two days or more.

Boat trips leave from both Porto and Vila Nova de Gaia. There are several companies to choose from and prices vary according to package. See www.douroacima.pt for some sample packages.

Espinho

Located about 15km (9 miles) south of Porto on the Atlantic coast, Espinho is a pretty seaside resort with pastel painted wooden houses and pedestrianised streets, where you can relax away from the city. There are beautiful beaches, water sports, golf and a casino. Places of interest include the ruins of the **Castro de Ovil**, dating back to the Iron Age.

Espinho is located just off the N109 south of Porto. Trains leave from Porto's São Bento and Campanhã Stations and take about 20 minutes.

Foz do Douro

If you want to get out of the city centre without straying too far, take tram No 18 to Foz do Douro at the mouth of the river. The tram runs along the seafront to the Castelo do Queijo, but you can get off before then and walk along the esplanade, stopping at a fish restaurant in Foz Velha.

Fundação Serralves

The Fundação Serralves in Porto is home to the 1930s' **Art Deco Casa de Serralves** and the **Museum of Contemporary Art**, designed by Alvaro Siza. There are also beautiful gardens, with formal areas and fountains, and a lake and pathways looking on to fields. A fabulous place to lose yourself and contemplate, read or just have afternoon tea.

See pp126–7.

Gaia

Vila Nova de Gaia is just across the river from Porto and has a few beaches where you can go to relax or do some surfing. The best beaches are **Francelos**, **Miramar**, **Aguda** and **Granja**.

You can either drive, taking the Ponte da Arrábida. Alternatively, take a train from São Bento Station in the centre of Porto, which takes 25–35 minutes, depending on the beach you choose.

Gondomar

Just 6km (3.5 miles) from Porto on the north side of the River Douro, Gondomar is renowned for its goldsmiths and particularly for its intricate filigree work. Although given city status in 1991, Gondomar is a very green place with rural traditions. Dating back to the 12th century, it has riverside 'beaches' where you can also go fishing, canoeing or take part in a river walk. From Monte Crasto, a hill in the centre of the parish, there are great views of Porto, Gaia and the surrounding area. *Take the EN209 from the southwest side of the Estrada da Circunvalação towards Gondomar.*

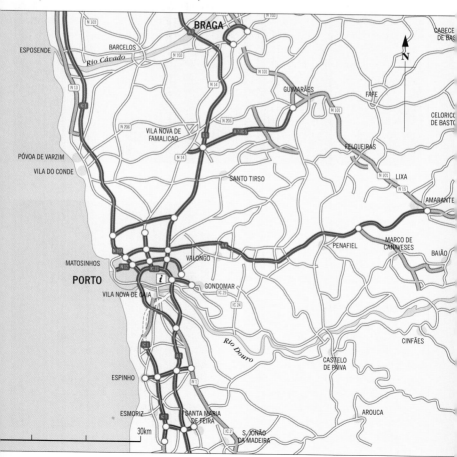

Douro valley near Pinhão

Matosinhos
Just north of Foz is the city of Matosinhos. There are beaches here, perhaps not the cleanest, but it is a good place to escape the city, and the fish restaurants on the seafront are fantastic.

Palácio de Cristal
The Palácio de Cristal is a great place to have lunch and a stroll in the park, with fabulous views over the River Douro and the city. Alternatively, you can end your day with a visit to the nearby **Museu Romântico** and **Solar do Vinho do Porto**, where you can relax in an armchair and sample the region's favourite export.
See p129.

You can visit the caves at Valongo

Parque da Cidade

Porto's largest park, located in Foz at the end of Avenida Boavista, the Parque da Cidade was first conceived in the 1960s but only opened as a public park in 1993. Covering 80 hectares of ground and with 10km of pathways, you can cycle or walk around the park where there are lakes and a large variety of flora and fauna.

Located in the west of the city, crossing the districts of Aldoar and Nevogilde. Until the metro is up and running it's best to go by car, taxi or bus. Bus: 19, 24 & 34.

Port Wine Tours

If you want to go to the heart of the Douro's green valleys, take a Port wine Tour and learn about the fortified wine. Routes can be followed by car, bus or boat, visiting the main urban centres as well as the vineyards. There are various routes available from any of the tourist bodies in the Douro Valley, either as organised tours or for you to follow independently at your leisure.
Porto Tourist Office: Rua Clube dos Fenianos (Central Tourist Office); tel: 22 339 3470. Rua do Infante D Henrique, 63; tel: 22 200 9770. Praça Dom João I; tel: 22 205 7514.
Diana Tours: Rua General Torres. Tel: 22 377 1230.
Rent a Cab: Rua Santa Catarina. Tel: 22 200 1530.

Valongo

This is a place of contrasts, a mixture of urban and rural environments, but what is interesting here is the Santa Justa Mountain, located nearby. As well as walks and more adventurous activities, there is a network of caves, a Palaeozoic park with preserved fossils and rare flora and fauna.
Located about 10km east of Porto just south of the A4-IP4.

Head for the beach at Foz after a walk in the Parque da Cidade

Shopping

Since the first shopping centres sprung up in the 1980s, spending a Saturday or Sunday at the mall has become a popular Portuguese pastime. There are also traditional shopping areas with everything from handmade goods to modern international boutiques. Many products are still cheaper than other European countries, and so shopping is an attractive prospect, and most credit cards are accepted at shops and ATMs.

Shop window display along Rua Santa Catarina, Porto

What to Buy

Apart from the clothing, music and household bargains you can find at the shopping centres, look out for *azulejos* (hand-painted tiles) and ceramics, copper utensils, lace, leather shoes, belts, bags and jewellery. If you want to splash out, there are designer shops and plenty of antiques. Wine lovers should not miss the quality selection on offer.

LISBON
Antiques
Rua Dom Pedro V, Rua do Chiado, Rua São Bento, Rua Pedro Alcântara.

Azulejos and Ceramics
Artesanato Português
Excellent selection of hand-painted tiles, plates and frames.
Rua Vieira Portuense, 34A – Belém. Open: daily 10am–7pm. Tel: 21 362 2117.
Fabrica de Ceramica Viuva Lamego
Largo do Intendente Pina Manique, 25. Tel: 21 885 2402; www.viuvalamego.com/.
Sant' Anna Addr.
Rua do Alecrim, 95–7. Tel: 21 363 8292.

Handicrafts
Artesanato Regional Português
Old handicraft shop with an impressive assortment of handmade goods.
Praça dos Restauradores, 64. Tel: 21 347 7875. Open: daily 9am–8pm.
Mercado da Ribeira
Run by the Lisbon Tourist Office and housed in the old wholesale food market, the market now sells handmade goods, regional cheese, wine and other food products and has occasional performances of folk music.
Avenida 24 de Julho (Cais do Sodré). Open: daily 10am–11pm (later Fri & Sat).
Santos Ofícios
Located in the Baixa, in a former Pombaline-era stable, this outlet sells a wide range of handmade products from all over the country.
Rua da Madalena, 87. Tel: 21 887 2031. Open: Mon–Sat 10am–8pm.

Markets
Feira da Ladra
Flea market in the Alfama district with a jumble of gems and junk.

Campo de Santa Clara. Open: Tue & Sat. Walk or take the 'scenic' tram No 28 from the Baixa.

Shopping Centres
Amoreiras
One of the older shopping centres with around 250 quality shops, a ten-screen cinema complex, supermarket, restaurants and parking facilities.
Rua Carlos Alberto da Mota Pinto/Avenida Engenheiro Duarte Pacheco. Open 10am–midnight. Tel: 21 381 0200.

Centro Comercial Vasco da Gama
Located in the Parque das Nações, this centre has vanguard architecture and design. In addition to the usual stores, there are terraces where you can enjoy a beer with views over the River Tagus.
Parque das Nações, Lisbon. Metro: Oriente.

Colombo
More than 400 stores selling both conservative styles and more funky fashion and clubbing wear. There is also a hypermarket, multi-screen cinema,

The Colombo (Lisbon) is the country's largest shopping centre

restaurants and underground parking facilities.
Avenida Lusíada (just off Avenida General Norton de Matos). Metro: Colégio Militar.

Portuguese Wines and Food
Coisas do Arco do Vinho
Located in the Belem Cultural Centre, it organises gastronomy and wine-related events and stocks a good range of wines for sale.
CCB, Rua Bartolomeu Dias, Loja 7/8. Tel: 21 364 2031. www.coisasdoarcodovinho.pt. Open: Tue–Sun 11am–8pm.
O Espírito do Vinho
Fantastic selection of the finest wines from Portugal and abroad.
Rua Ferreira Borges, 94B. Tel: 21 386 7791. Open: 10.30am–8pm.

Traditional Shopping Areas
The **Baixa**, **Avenida da Roma**, **Alvalade** and **Campo de Ourique** all have the international stores found in the shopping centres plus a good selection of local products such as leather and jewellery. For designer goods head for Avenida da Liberdade and the Chiado.

LISBON SHOPPING CARD

Available from the tourist offices, once the card is validated it gives 5–20 per cent discount at around 200 stores in the Baixa, Chiado and Avenida da Liberdade.

The cost depends on whether you want to shop until you drop (24 or 72 hours), but it is good value.

Traditional shopping in Rue Santa Catarina

PORTO
Books and Music
FNAC Stores
Located at most commercial centres and areas, these stores stock a wide range of titles and have a foreign language section, music, and a café where you can browse through the books.
Livraria Bertrand
Portuguese chain of bookstores which also stock a small selection of books in English.
Rua 31 de Janeiro, 65. Tel: 22 200 4339.
Livraria Lello & Irmão
Founded in 1906, this is Porto's best independent bookstore, worth visiting just for the building.
Rua das Carmelitas, 144. Tel: 22 200 2037.

Handicrafts
Armazém dos Linhos
Sells a good selection of linen and regional woven fabrics.
Rua de Passos Manuel, 19. Tel: 22 200 4750.
Galeria de Artesanato 'O Galo'
A good place to buy decorative ceramics, it also has a permanent exhibition.

Rua Mouzinho da Silveira, 68. Tel: 22 332 5294.

Markets
Bolhão
Traditional old fruit and vegetable market that also sells cheese, pulses, meat, live chickens and plants.
Rua de Sá da Bandeira. Open: Mon–Fri 8am–5pm, Sat 8am–1pm.

Shopping Centres
Arrábida Shopping Centre
Located over the Arrábida Bridge on the Vila Nova da Gaia side of the Douro, this shopping centre is one of the largest in the Porto area. It has two floors of shops, restaurants and cinemas. The restaurant area has fabulous views over the Douro.
Praceta José F Caldas.
Norte Shopping
Located closer to Matosinhos, this is an impressive shopping centre with all the usual suspects, plus a large selection of eateries.
Rua Sara Afonso.
Shopping Via Catarina
If you want to mix traditional street shopping areas with contemporary malls, this is a good option.
Rua Santa Catarina, 312.

Portuguese Wines and Food
Casa Oriental
Sells a great selection of groceries and bacalhau.
Campo dos Mártires da Pátria, 110–12. Tel: 22 200 2530.
Confeitaria Cunha
Fantastic cake and chocolate shop, which will have you salivating. There is

also a café and a restaurant at the back.
Rua Sá da Bandeira. Tel: 22 200 4469.

Garrafeira do Carmo
Founded in 1990, this specialist wine
shop has vintages from harvests as far
back as the early 20th century.
Rua do Carmo, 17–18. Tel: 22 200 3285.

Garrafeira do Infante
This Port wine shop in the Ribeira caters
for the tourist and wines are expensive.
However, you can taste as many as you
like, which is a bonus.
Rua Infante Dom Henrique, 83–5.
Tel: 22 208 4493.

Traditional Shopping Areas
Rua Santa Catarina has a traditional
shopping area and the Via Catarina
Shopping Centre, with international
stores and traditional shops. There are
a large number of shoe shops in this
area too and in **Rua Passos Manuel**.
Other traditional shopping alternatives
are **Rua de Cedofeita** and the **Boavista**
area, particularly along **Rua de Júlio
Dinis**.

TOP TIP

For a good selection of wines and Port,
head for one of the large supermarkets or
specialist stores in the shopping centres. The
price is much more attractive and you can also
buy cheeses, *presunto* (cured ham), coffee and
olive oil, and other local food products, all
with their distinct local flavours.

Fish vendors sell from street stalls in Lisbon

Entertainment

Both Lisbon and Porto's cultural scenes have been boosted by their recent status of European Cities of Culture. While Lisbon's activities have rocketed with the building of the Centro Cultural de Belém and the Parque das Nações, Porto has the fabulous Fundação Serralves and awaits the completion of the Casa da Música. You can get a good overview of what's on before you go by visiting *www.whatsonwhen.com*.

There is a wide range of entertainment on offer

Poster advertising one of the many exhibitions at the Centro Cultural de Belém

LISBON
Art Galleries
Antiks Pinturas
Exhibits 19th-century paintings by Portuguese masters and a good collection of contemporary jewellery.
Rua S. Bento, 199 – B, Loja 7. Tel: 21 395 4742. Open: Mon–Fri 11am–1pm & 3–7pm.

Galeria 111
Wide selection of work by modern Portuguese artists.
Campo Grande, 113. Tel: 21 797 7418. Open: Mon–Sat 10am–1pm & 3–7pm.

Galeria São Mamede
Good collection of modern classics.
Rua Escola Politécnica, 167. Tel: 21 397 3255. Open: 10.30am–1pm & 3–7.30pm. Closed Mon morning.

Santos & Marcos, Lda
This gallery specialises in Spanish and Portuguese colonial art.
Rua Dom Pedro V, 59. Tel: 21 342 6367.

Theatre
Unless you are a good Portuguese speaker, the language barrier will prove a problem. However, there are many theatres, including fringe ones. Tickets are available from the box offices and some from **FNAC stores**.

Centro Cultural de Belém
The CCB hosts a wide variety of performances from concerts and ballet to theatre.
Praça do Império. www.ccb.pt.

Teatro Aberto
Fringe theatre with performances by the resident Novo Grupo de Teatro, and companies from around the country and overseas.

Praça de Espanha. Tel: 21 797 0969. www.teatroaberto.com.

Teatro Camões
This large theatre in the Parque das Nações was designed to host major musical, dance and theatrical events and is home to the Orquestra Sinfónica Portuguesa (Portuguese Symphony Orchestra).
Parque das Nações. Tel: 21 896 6599. www.parquedasnacoes.pt/touristguide/.

Teatro da Trindade
The Teatro Aberto in the Bairro Alto presents theatrical performances, musicals and concerts.
Largo da Trindade, 7A. Tel: 21 342 3200. www.teatrotrindade.inatel.pt.

Teatro Nacional D Maria II
This beautiful theatre shows major productions of theatre, circus and performance art.
Praça do Rossio. Tel: 21 342 2210. www.teatro-dmaria.pt.

Teatro Politeama
Features musical productions and plays.
Rua das Portas de S Antão, 119. Tel: 21 343 1200.

Cinema
The *Diário de Notícias* newspaper or *cinema.sapo.pt* (search by city) have film listings, and there are multiplexes at all of the large shopping centres. Most films are shown in the original language with Portuguese subtitles. The **Londres cinema** (*Avenida da Roma, 7A*) shows art house films.

LISBON MUSIC
There is a wealth of music on offer in Lisbon. It boasts the country's premier orchestra and ballet (The Gulbenkian,

see pp46–7) and welcomes visits by internationally renowned conductors, orchestras and ballet companies throughout the concert season.

From the Alfama to the Bairro Alto, Lisbon is also known for its fado houses, where you can eat, drink and listen to the Portuguese 'blues' (*see pp48–9*).

The city also has several jazz venues, from the legendary **Hot Clube de Portugal** to the **Speakeasy**.

Concert Halls
Centro Cultural de Belém
See p38.
Coliseu dos Recreios
Originally built in 1890, the Coliseum was renovated in 1994 when Lisbon was European City of Culture. It hosts both classical and popular music concerts.
Rua Portas de Santo Antão.
Tel: 21 346 1997.
Grande and Pequeno Auditório at the Fundação Calouste Gulbenkian
At the Gulbenkian's large auditorium you can see its own orchestra, choir and ballet, and visiting orchestras.
Avenida da Berna, 45. Tel: 21 782 3030.
www.gulbenkian.pt.
Pavilhão Atlântico
In addition to concerts and operas, the Atlantic Pavilion hosts international sports events and shows for children.
Alameda dos Oceanos.
www.pavilhaoatlantico.pt/.
Teatro Nacional São Carlos
The Teatro Nacional São Carlos stages operas and classical music.
Rua Serpa Pinto, 9. Tel: 21 346 8408.

Please note the star-rating system applied below:
*   under €20
**   from €20–25
***   over €25.

Fado and Folk Music
Adegas Mesquita**
Located in the heart of the Bairro Alto, the traditional fado atmosphere is found in this restaurant, along with tasty Portuguese cuisine.
Rua Diário de Notícias, 107.
Tel: 21 321 9280. Open: daily 8pm–2am.
Arcadas do Faia.***
This is an expensive place to listen to fado, but you will get a generous serving of Lisbon fado and quality Portuguese cooking in the heart of the Bairro Alto.
Rua Barroca, 54/56. Tel: 21 342 6742.
Open: daily 8pm–2am.
Café Luso**
One of Lisbon's oldest and most typical restaurants and fado houses, dating back to 1927.
Travessia da Queimada, 10. Tel: 21 342 2281. Open: Mon–Sat 8pm–3am.
Clube de Fado**
Rua S João da Praça, 92–4 (Nr Sé).
Tel: 21 885 2704. Open: Mon–Sat 7pm–3am.
Noites de Luar**
As well as fado you might hear a little bossa nova and other Brazilian rhythms.
Beco Bombarda, 4 at Rua Bombarda.
Tel: 21 315 8194. Open: Mon–Sat 7pm–3am. Closed Sun.

The Calouste Gulbenkian Foundation's auditorium, set in beautiful grounds

Estoril's famous casino offers a great evening's entertainment

Jazz
Bar do Terraço
At the Centro Cultural de Belém you can listen to free jazz on the terrace during the summer.
Praça do Império. Tel: 21 301 0623. Open: Mon–Fri 12.30–9.30pm, Sat & Sun 12.30–7pm.
Hot Clube de Portugal**
Lisbon's famous jazz basement, located next to its own jazz school, hosts concerts by different bands every Friday and Saturday.
Praça da Alegria, 39. Tel: 21 346 7369. Open: Tue–Sat 10pm–2am.
Joke**
Live bossa nova and jazz from Wednesday to Sunday.

Rua Frei Miguel Contreiras, 18C. Tel: 21 849 9081. Open: Wed–Sun 11pm–3am.
Speakeasy**
This riverfront restaurant has live music every night from 11pm, but is particularly busy at the weekends.
Cais Oficinas, Rocha Conde Obidos. Tel: 21 396 4257. Open: Mon–Sat 8pm–4am.

LISBON NIGHTLIFE
The traditional places for Lisbon's nightlife are in the Chiado and the Bairro Alto, or even out of town in the resort of Cascais. However, these places now attract more tourists than genuine Lisboetas. In the past few years, warehouses on the riverfront have been

converted into clubs and restaurants and now the Alcântara is *the* place to go.

Casinos
Estoril Casino

This is the biggest casino in Europe, but you do not necessarily have to gamble your money away. There are substantial gaming rooms and leisure facilities, but the casino also offers a great dinner and show ticket.

Praça José Teodoro dos Santos, 2765–237, Estoril. Tel: 21 466 7700.

Dancing and Popular Music
B. leza

Popular with an older crowd, this venue is located inside a 16th-century palace and plays African and Latin American rhythms. There are often live bands.

Largo Conde Barão, 50. Tel: 21 396 3735. Open: Tue–Sat 10.30pm–7am.

Bipi-Bipi

Live Brazilian (*brazuca*) music and caipirinhas.

Rua Oliveira Martins, 6 E. Tel: 21 797 8924. Open: Mon–Sat 10.30pm–2am.

BiStyle

The older crowd come from 6–10pm for cheese and wine, and then the younger crowd dance the night away to 1980s' rock.

Rua Prior Crato, 6. Tel: 21 397 3303. Open: Mon–Sat 10.30pm–2am.

Blues Café

This restaurant-cum-rock and blues joint is one of the cool places to hang out.

Doca de Alcântara. Tel: 21 397 7085. Open: Mon–Thur 8pm–4am, Fri & Sat 8pm–5am.

The Hot Clube is the place for jazz in Lisbon

Fado is a serious business

Jamaica
Reggae, 1960s' and 1970s' music every
Tuesday night.
*Rua Nova Carvalho. Tel: 21 342 1859.
Open: Mon–Sat 11pm–4am.*

Johnny Guitar
Live bands play here most nights.
*Calçada Marquês Abrantes, 72. Tel: 21
396 0415. Open: Mon–Thur
11pm–3.30am, Fri & Sat midnight–4am.*

Paradise Garage
Many up-and-coming bands play at this
dockside venue.
*Rua João de Oliveira Miguéns, 38/48.
Tel: 21 395 7157. Open: Mon–Sat.
Concerts generally at 9pm, open till late.*

Rock City
American bar with live music and rock
'n' roll memorabilia on sale.

*Rua Cintura Porto Lisboa, Armazém, 225.
Tel: 21 342 8640. Open: 12.30pm–4am.*

PORTO
Art Galleries
arthobler.com
This art gallery exhibits work by the
new vanguard artists.
*Rua Miguel Bombarda. Tel: 22 608 4448.
www.arthobler.com.*

Auditório Casa das Artes
This is more of a cultural centre with
collective exhibitions.
Ruben A, 210. Tel: 22 600 4301.

Cooperativa Arvore
Opened in 1963 by a group of vanguard
artists with a dream of freedom of
expression, the Cooperativa Arvore
survived harsh opposition and physical

attacks in the 1960s and 1970s. It even made more space available to lithographers, photographers and ceramic artists. Today it also hosts temporary exhibitions, round-table discussions and other events.
Rua Azevedo de Albuquerque, 1. Tel: 22 207 6010. www.arvorecoop.pt/. Open: Mon–Fri 9am–11pm, Sat 3–5pm & 9.30–11pm, Sun 3–8pm. Buses: 3, 18, 20 & 35.

Galeria Arte & Manifesto
Exhibits all kinds of Portuguese and international artwork.

Rua do Breiner, 346. Tel: 22 208 0553. Open: Mon–Fri 10am–12.30pm, Sat 2.30–7pm.

Galeria Módulo
This gallery has contemporary art with a focus on work by Portuguese artists. There is also a selection of photography.
Avenida da Boavista, 854. Tel: 22 609 4742. Open: Mon–Sat 3–8pm.

Galeria Símbolo
Exhibits contemporary sculpture and painting.
Rua da Cedofeita. Tel: 22 205 6552. Open: Mon–Sat 3–8pm.

Porto's Teatro Nacional de São Carlos

The Coliseu do Porto offers everything from concerts to circuses

Galeria Vertag

This gallery has a collection of contemporary design.
Avenida da Boavista, 1635. Tel: 22 617 1314. Open: Mon–Fri 9am–12.30pm & 2–6pm.

Theatre
Rivoli Teatro Municipal

Presents a wide range of national and international dance and theatrical productions.
Praça Dom João I. Tel: 22 339 2200.

Teatro do Campo Alegre

National and international theatre and dance productions.
Rua das Estrelas. Tel: 22 606 3000.

Teatro Helena Sá e Costa

Fringe theatre with good, mostly Portuguese, productions.
Rua da Alegria, 503. Tel: 22 518 9982.

Teatro Nacional São João

One of Porto's most important theatres, the São João stages theatre, music, dance and puppetry by national and international artists.
Praça da Batalha. Tel: 22 340 1910. www.tnsj.pt.

Cinema

The *Diário de Notícias* newspaper or *cinema.sapo.pt/* (search by city) have film listings and there are multiplexes at all of the large shopping centres. Most films are shown in the original language with Portuguese subtitles. Check *www.agendadporto.pt* for more art house films.

PORTO MUSIC

Since 2001, Porto's cultural scene has lifted. As it awaits the completion of the Casa da Música, there are still plenty of places to listen to jazz, see a symphony orchestra or laugh at a comical play.

Concert Halls
Auditorio do Museu de Arte Contemporaneo (Serralves)

The auditorium hosts classical music concerts and jazz.
Rua Dom João de Castro. Tel: 22 615 6500. www.serralves.pt.

Casa das Artes

Shows audio-visual events, traditional music performances and discussion groups, as well as other arty events.
Rua António Cardoso 175. Tel: 22 600 4301.

Coliseu do Porto
Presents a variety of performances
from orchestras, operas and ballets
to contemporary bands and dance
performances.
*Rua Passos Manuel, 137. Tel: 22 339
4940. www.coliseudporto.pt.*
Mosteiro de São Bento
Currently home to the Orquestra
Nacional do Porto until the completion
of the Casa da Música, it hosts various
concert performances throughout the
year.
*Rua de São Bento da Vitória. Tel: 22 207
4940.*
Teatro Nacional de São Carlos
See p66.

Fado and Folk Music
See pp163–71.

Jazz
Café da Praça
There is live jazz here every Sunday
night and DJs throughout the week.
*Praça de Lisboa, 16. Tel: 22 208 6498.
Open: Tue–Sat 6pm–3am.*

PORTO NIGHTLIFE
Dancing and Popular Music
Anikibóbó
This veteran bar-club attracts all age
groups to drink or dance.
*Fonte Taurina, 36–8. Tel: 22 332 4619.
Open: Thur–Sat 9pm–4am.*
Foz Brasil
Mansion-size club with various theme-
oriented rooms, mostly with Brazilian
rhythms because it is owned by
Brazilian footballer Edmilson.
Avenida do Brasil, Mansão do Castelo.

*Tel: (22) 600 2422. Open: Tue–Sat
7pm–3am.*
Hard Club
Live music venue that has all the latest
up-and-coming bands.
*Cais de Gaia. Tel: 22 375 3819. Open:
Wed–Sat 10pm–4am.*
Indústria
Fashionable nightclub that plays dance
music and gets very crowded at the
weekends.
*C. C.l da Fez, Avenida do Brasil, 843 AF.
Tel: 22 617 6806.*
Via Invicta Capital Samba
Live Brazilian music and caipirinhas to
make you dance.
*Delfim Ferreira, 564. Tel: 22 610 8172.
Open: Thur–Sat 9pm–4am.*

Up-and-coming bands at the Hard Club

Children

The Portuguese love children and do not exclude them from all their 'adult' activities. Children tend to accompany the family wherever they go, and at the weekend this often involves a shopping centre. At the same time, they still have a long childhood, and are involved in sports and other activities with their friends.

Some parks have play areas for children

Here are a few suggestions on how to keep your children occupied.

LISBON
Children's Museum
Children aged 4–13 can have fun and learn here with games and interactive discovery.
Praça do Império, Museu da Marinha. Tel: 21 386 4923. Open: Tue–Sun 10am–6pm. Tram: 15. Buses: 27, 28 & 29.

Museu da Marioneta
This museum will delight children who like puppets. Not only are there hundreds of them on show, but children can watch puppet shows on video and learn how the production machinery works.
Convento das Bernardas, Rua da Esperança, 146. Tel: 21 394 2810.

Parque das Nações
The Nation's Park is a good place to spend the day with the children. As well as the Aquarium, cable car, Vasco da Gama Tower and Knowledge Pavilion, there are outdoor play parks and a bowling alley. You can hire bicycles for adults and children close to the Pavilhão Atlântico. (*See pp72–3.*)

Shopping Centres
Although this is a national pastime, you might want to leave shopping for a rainy weekday, as the malls can get very crowded. However, inside there are shops, games machines and cinemas to keep the kids out of trouble, and all the kinds of foods they beg for all year round.

Zoo Lisboa
Lisbon's zoo has a wide range of animals that will please the children at feeding time, ranging from big cats, buffalos and camels to parrots and other kinds of tropical birds.

There are also reptiles, including alligators and crocodiles. In addition to recreating a tropical environment, there are playgrounds and numerous rides and activities.
Estrada de Benfica. Tel: 21 723 2900. Open: 10am–6pm. Metro: Jardim.

PORTO
Epicentro
This arts centre is aimed at 5–10 year olds. If you are around for a while and the weather is bad, why not enrol them in an arts workshop.
Caminho da Fonte de Cima, 33. Tel 22 616 8749. Open: Mon–Sat 3–7.30pm.

Parks

Parks are often a good place to take children because they have play areas and often organised activities. The **Palácio de Cristal** has a good play area and at the **Parque da Cidade** the children can feed the ducks on the lakes, ride their bikes or fly kites. It is better for children to be accompanied by an adult because some of the parks are very big and can be a little isolated. (*See pp138–9.*)

Portugal dos Pequeninhos

Located close to Coimbra, this is a great place to take the kids if you want a proper day trip out of the city or are travelling between Porto and Lisbon. This is a 'mini-Portugal', showing both its architecture and folklore on a small scale that appeals to children. Adults can have fun here too.
Largo do Rossio – Santa Clara. Tel: 23 944 1225. Open: Mar–May, 10am–7pm, June–Sept, 9am–8pm, Sept–Dec, 10am–5pm. Closed 25 Dec.

Shopping Centres

As for Lisbon. Also Norte Shopping (*Rua Sara Afonso, Matosinhos; tel: 22 954 7171*) has a bowling alley.

Torre dos Clérigos

Although many children like the idea of climbing to the top of a tower, it is probably not wise if they are too small because there are too many steps and nooks and crannies to fall down.
Rua São Felipe de Nery, Porto. Tel: 22 200 1729.

Or take the cheeky monkeys to the zoo

Sport and Leisure

The Portuguese love their football, whether the local team or the national selection. With the hosting of the European Cup in 2004, this will be taken to the extreme. Apart from football, there are opportunities for all kinds of sports from roller hockey and basketball to mountain biking, surfing and, of course, plenty of golf.

Rather than two separate city listings, sports are ordered by discipline.

Benfica pennant

Adventure Activities

There are numerous companies that offer weekend breaks for activities from canoeing and kayaking to climbing, mountain biking, four-wheel drive and white water rafting. Whatever your choice, they will usually tailor the trip according to duration and number of participants, and take you out to the natural parks. The following are examples of companies that offer such trips.

Arrábida Aventuras
Estrada Barris, Palmela, Lisbon. Tel: 21 233 6113. www.arrabida-aventuras.com/.

Ecoturismo Montanha Viva
Desporto Aventura e Protecção Ambiental, Rua Padre Arieira, 292, São Torcato, 4800 Guimarães. Tel: 25 355 3139.

Bowling

BIL
This large bowling venue in Lisbon's ultra-modern Parque das Nações has 30 'alleys' as well as snooker, bars, fast food and party rooms for hire.
Avenida dos Oceanos (close to Vasco da Gama shopping centre). Mon–Thur noon–2am, Fri noon–4am, Sat 11–4am, Sun & public holidays 11–2am.

Canoeing

Arrábida Aventuras
Lisbon. Tel: 21 235 2406. www.arrabida-aventuras.com/.

Federação Portuguesa de Canoagem
Rua António Pinto Machado, 60–3º (D3), 4100-068 Porto. Tel: 22 606 6227.

Football (Soccer)

The main teams in Lisbon are Sporting and Benfica, while in Porto there is FC Porto, and also Boavista. Check for more information at *www.fpf.pt/.*

Golf

Portugal has long been a popular destination for golf. Although more people go to the Algarve, there are several top courses in and around Lisbon.

Belas Clube de Campo
Just 20 minutes drive from Lisbon in the Sintra hills, this course has five lakes and an undulating layout. There is an 18-hole course with a par 72 layout, driving range and two practice putting greens.
Alameda do Aqueduto, Belas Clube de Campo, Belas. Tel: (21) 962 6640. www.belasgolf.com/.

Club de Golf do Estoril
World-renowned course by the resort of
Estoril. Eighteen holes for a par of 69.
Sea views, driving range, putting green
and leisure facilities.
Avenida da Republica, Estoril.
Tel: 21 468 0176.

Oitavos Golf
A 30-minute drive from Lisbon by the
Sintra hills, amongst pine trees and sand
dunes with views of the Atlantic Ocean.
An 18-hole course with a par 71 layout,
driving range, putting greens and
chipping areas.
Quinta da Marinha, Casa da Quinta, 25,
Cascais. Tel: 21 486 0000.

There are also various golf courses
around Porto.

Estela Golf Course
Located on the Minho coast, close
to Póvoa de Varzim, this new 18-hole
course for a par of 72 can get misty
in the mornings but clears by the
afternoon.
Rua Rio Alto, 4570–242 Estela.
Tel: 25 260 1567.

Miramar Golf Club
This is a small course close to Espinho.
With nine holes for a par of 34, it is one
of Portugal's oldest.
Praia da Miramar, 4405–591 Valadares,
Tel: 22 762 2067.

Lisbon Marathon

Be careful not to capsize!

Porto Golf Club
Also close to Espinho and the coastline, this is an 18-hole course for a par of 71, and one of the oldest and most traditional in Europe.
Estrada de Paramos, 4500–520 Paramos. Tel: 22 734 2008.

Horse Racing
Hipodromo do Campo Grande
Located by the University of Lisbon campus, this racetrack hosts event races throughout the year.
1600 Lisboa. Tel: 21 793 4334. Metro: Campo Grande and Cidade Universitária.

Mountain Biking
Adventure companies often organise cycling tours, but there are also specialist cycling and rent-a-bike companies.

Omni Surf Shop
Rua do Poço, 38–42, 4900 Viana do Castelo. Tel: 25 882 0024.
Tejo Bike
To right of flags by Pavilhão Atlântico, Parque das Nações, Lisbon.
Trilhos
Rua de Belém, 94, 4300 Porto. Tel: 22 550 4604.

Swimming
Campanhã (Municipal)
Rua Dr. Sousa Ávides, Porto. Tel: 22 537 2041.
Constituição (Municipal)
Rua Almirante Leote do Rego (G4), Porto. Tel: 22 550 6601.
Piscina do Ateneu
Rua das Portas de Santo Antao 102, Rossio, Lisbon. Tel: (21) 343 0947.

Tennis

There are both sports centres and specialised tennis clubs.

Centro de Tenis das Olaias
Rua Robalo Gouveia, Lisbon.
Tel: 21 840 7130. Metro: Olaias.

Clube de Ténis do Porto
Terrenos anexos à Rua Damião de Góis (G3), 4050-227 Porto. Tel: 22 502 8506.

Water Sports

There are numerous water-based sports around both Lisbon and Porto. Obviously the resorts have various companies and activities, including windsurfing, canoeing, diving and sailing, however, within the cities there are ample opportunities too.

Lisbon Oceanarium Sea Club
Doca dos Olivais, Parque das Nações, Lisbon. Tel: 21 891 8532.

Sport Club do Porto
Rua de Santa Catarina, 132–r/c (H2), Porto. Tel: 22 200 1785.

The delights of outdoor swimming

Food and Drink

The Portuguese are great lovers of food and their generous portions reflect this. As well as various meat dishes, the Atlantic seaboard supplies an almost equal number of seafood meals. In the north, there are more pork and kid dishes and, of course, Porto is renowned for its tripe. However, you can easily avoid this and opt for a dish of stuffed squid legs or grilled sardines.

Dried salt cod fish on sale

Lisbon also has its fair share of seafood dishes, with crab and prawns high on the menu beside beef and veal. Along with bacalhau (see opposite), soup is the mainstay of many Portuguese meals, particularly *caldo verde* (cabbage soup). However, this is often flavoured with chicken stock and chopped *chouriço* (spicy sausage) so it is not a vegetarian option. Non-meat eaters will face a few obstacles in the food department, but globalisation means that the restaurants are more internationalised, particularly in Lisbon, and do cater for vegetarians. There are also a large number of sweets made from eggs, from the famous *pasteis de nata* to *flan*.

Fish forms a significant part of the Portuguese diet

RECIPE

Bacalhau com natas – salt cod fish with cream and potatoes

Portugal has more than 1,000 salt cod recipes. One of the most popular and delicious is bacalhau com natas, served with cream and potatoes.

Ingredients

600g (20oz) salt cod fish (soak overnight)

2 medium onions

30g (1oz) plain flour

30g (1oz) butter

1.5l milk

0.25l cream (in Portugal you can buy this in powdered form)

1 bay leaf

Salt and pepper

1 or 2 cloves garlic

½kg (2.2lb) potatoes

Cut the fish into chunks and rinse in clean water several times before cooking in a pan with fresh water until it becomes tender. Cut the onions finely and the potato in thin slices. Then fry them lightly in oil. Melt the butter, adding the flour until it becomes a ball. Add the milk little by little, mixing constantly. When it becomes liquid, add a little salt and pepper and the cream, giving it a thick creamy consistency. Reheat the onions and potato and add the fish, letting them heat gently for a while. Put a knob of butter in an ovenproof dish and add the potato and fish mixture. Then pour the creamy sauce over it and put in the oven at a high to medium heat until it is browned.
www.gastronomias.com/receitas/rec0117.htm (Roteiro Gastronómico de Portugal, ©Arte Digital, Lda)

Typical Dishes and Specialities

Soups (Caldos)
Caldo verde: Cabbage soup.
Sopa Alentejana: Garlic and bread soup.
Sopa de Feijão verde: Green bean soup.
Sopa de Legumes: Vegetable soup.

STARTERS

When you enter some restaurants, the waiter often places a basket of bread and a selection of cheeses or other snacks on the table. If you eat these, they will be added on to the bill. If you do not want them, ask for them to be taken away.

Main Courses
Bife tornedo: Large succulent piece of beef usually served rare.
Bifes de Perú: Turkey steak.
Cabrito assado: Grilled kid.
Carne de vaca assada: Roast meat.
Costeleta de Vitela: Veal cutlets/chops.

Frango assado: Baked or grilled chicken.
Frango no churrasco: Barbecued chicken.
Leitão assado: Suckling pig.
Lombo de porco assado: Pork roast.
Tripas à moda do Porto: Typical tripe dish from Porto flavoured with cumin, black pepper, sausage and chicken.

Fish
Amêijoas a bolhão: Cockles in olive oil with a squeeze of lemon.
Amêijoas na Cataplana: Cockles with sausage and smoked ham.
Bacalhau: There are more than 1,000 recipes. Ask the restaurant what is in it.
Caldeirada: Fish stew.
Camarão: Prawns.
Espada: Swordfish.
Gambas grelhadas: Grilled king prawns.
Linguado: Sole.
Lulas recheadas: Stuffed squid.
Pescada: Hake.
Polvo grelhado: Grilled octopus.
Sardinhas assadas: Grilled sardines.

Vegetables
Azeitonas: Olives.
Batatas: Potatoes.

Batatas fritas: Chips.
Ervilhas: Peas.
Espinafres: Spinach.
Salada Mixta: Green salad.
Tomate: Tomato.

Dessert
Bolinhos de mel: Honey cakes.
Bolo rei: Portuguese Christmas cake with dried fruit.
Doces: Sweets.
Gelados: Ice cream.
Mousse de Chocolate: Chocolate mousse.
Pão de ló: Typical northern Easter cake made with a light sponge.
Papos de Anjo: Egg-based pastry dish.
Pasteis de nata: Portuguese custard tart.
Pudim: Crème caramel.

Cheese
Queijo cabra: Goat's cheese
Queijo de vaca e ovelha: Cow and sheep's milk cheese.

Fruit
Ananas: Pineapple.
Banana: Banana.
Laranja: Orange.
Maçã: Apple.
Melão: Melon.
Morango: Strawberry.
Uvas: Grapes.

BANANAS

If you order a banana for pudding, it will be served on a plate with a knife and fork. The Portuguese are quite adept at skinning and eating the fruit with their cutlery and it is considered polite. However, as a tourist you are forgiven for ripping the thing open and taking a big bite.

Snacks and Cakes
Francesinha: Typical evening snack in Porto, it is like a ham, steak and cheese sandwich with a seafood and brandy sauce poured over the top.
Omeleta: Omelette.
Tosta Mixta: Toasted ham and cheese sandwich.

Other
Broa: Corn-based bread, typical of the north.
Chá: Tea (you have to ask for milk).
Espetada: Anything cooked on a spit.
Fiambre: Ham.
Leite: Milk.
Maionese: Mayonnaise.
Pão: Bread.
Presunto: Portuguese cured ham.
Queijo: Cheese.
Sandes: Sandwich.

There are plenty of sweet things on sale, such as dried and crystallised fruit

Where to Eat

In Lisbon, the Bairro Alto and the Chiado have always been the usual places to eat. You can still eat well here at traditional restaurants, fado houses, *cevejarías* (beer houses that serve steak or seafood and chips) and *tascas* (cheap restaurants). However, modernisation of the city means that new eateries have sprung up with more international styles of eating. In the Parque das Nações, there are a large number of restaurants, many with views of the river. The real development in terms of social life is the old dock area on the banks of the Tagus, particularly in the Alcântara district.

Shopping centres are also a surprisingly good option in both Lisbon and Porto, especially if you are on the move. Half a floor may be given over to restaurants and snack bars, offering everything from typical Portuguese food in decent restaurants, weigh-and-pay Brazilian buffet-style eateries, sandwich and burger bars, and coffees and pastries.

Porto may not have as many restaurants as Lisbon, but it has its own offering of traditional food from the region. There are a few fado restaurants in the Ribeira, but development here has seen new modern restaurants open up, catering for both tourists and the arty crowds. While in Porto, it is worth heading to Foz, at the mouth of the Douro, where there is an

Restaurant in the Museu Nacional do *Azulejos*

abundance of good fish restaurants.

Portuguese like to drink wine with their meals, to complement whatever food they are eating. Beer is on offer as well, especially in the cheaper restaurants and the *cevejarías*.

Prices have gone up since Portugal joined the European Union in 1986, and again since the introduction of the Euro in 2001. Nevertheless, it is still possible to eat really well at a reasonable price and, unlike many European cities, you are not charged extortionate prices for coffee and cakes. Of course, there are more upmarket restaurants both in and

outside Lisbon and Porto, places where the service is impeccable and you get your money's worth. For these, make a reservation to avoid disappointment.

Please note the star-rating system applied below: * under €20, ** from €20–25, *** over €25.

LISBON RESTAURANTS
Portuguese Cuisine
A Travessa**
Fresh fish and fine Portuguese cooking, with mussels on Saturday nights.
*Travessa do Convento das Bernardas, 12.
Tel: 21 390 2034. Open Mon–Sat 12.30–3pm & 8pm–midnight.*

Belcanto***
Classic Lisbon restaurant, famous for its egg dish *Ovos a Professor*. A restaurant aimed at businesspeople – the waiters can be very rude to 'scruffy tourists'.
Largo de São Carlos, 10. Tel: 21 342 0607. Open daily 12–5pm & 7–11pm.
Casa de Leão***
Good for a business lunch or intimate evening, with great views over the city.
Castelo de São Jorge. Tel: 21 887 5962. Open: daily 12.30–3pm & 8–10pm.
Cervejaria Trindade*
Beautiful old canteen used by the Trinos Monks from 1283–1755, when the Great Earthquake damaged it. Opened as a *cevejarías* in the 19th century, it is covered in *azulejos*. Great for steaks and seafood with a beer or two.
Rua Nova da Trindade 20. Tel: 21 342 3506. Open: daily 9–2am.
Cozinha Velha***
Located in the old palace kitchen at Queluz, this is a superb restaurant in luxurious surroundings, perfect for a little romance or even a business lunch.

Azulejos feature in restaurants too

Largo do Palácio, Queluz.
Tel: 21 435 6158. Open:
daily 12.30–3pm &
7.30–10pm.
Doca 6*
Fresh fish and shellfish.
Doca de Santo Amaro,
Armazém 6. Tel: 21 395
7905. Open: Mon–Fri
12.30–3pm &
7.30pm–midnight,
Sat–Sun 12.30–3.30pm
& 7.30pm–midnight.
Faz Figura*
Portuguese cuisine with
a few international dishes
and a great view over
the river.
Rua do Paraíso (Parque
das Nações), 15B.
Tel: 21 886 8981.
Open: Mon–Sat 12.30–3pm
& 8pm–midnight.
Jardim do Marisco*
Fresh fish and seafood.
Avenida Infante Dom
Henrique, Doca do
Bacalhau, Pavilhão A/B
(Parque das Nações). Tel:
21 882 4240. Open: daily
12.30–3pm & 8–10pm.
Mãe d'Agua*
Located above the
aqueduct, this restaurant
has fabulous views over
the city.
Jardim Amoreiras.
Tel: 21 385 8743.
Open: 4pm–2am.
Pap'Acorda*
One of the most famous
restaurants in Lisbon.
Rua da Atalaia, 57–9.
Tel: 21 346 4811. Open:
Tue–Sat 12.30–2.30pm
& 8–11pm.
Páteo Alfacinha*
Traditional Portuguese
cooking with folk music
and dance.
Rua do Guarda Jóias, 44.
Tel: 21 364 2171. Open:
daily 10am–midnight.
Restaurante Veranda*
Fine Portuguese food
with a view over the city,
as well as live music and
dancing on Wednesday to
Saturday evenings.
D Duarte, 4–8° (inside
Hotel Mundial). Tel: 21
886 3101. Open: daily
noon–3.30pm &
7.30–10.30pm.
Tertúlia do Tejo*
Both Portuguese and
international dishes.
Fresh fish and seafood.
Doca de Santo Amaro,
Pavilhão 4. Tel: 21 395
5552. Open: noon–3pm
& 7–11.15pm.

Fado restaurant in Lisbon

Fado Restaurants
Adegas Mesquita*
Traditional fado
atmosphere with tasty
Portuguese cuisine.
*Rua Diário de Notícias,
107. Tel: 21 321 9280.
Open: Mon–Sat 8pm–late.*
Arcadas do Faia*
Expensive but good
place to listen to fado and
try Portuguese cooking.
*Rua da Barroca 54–6.
Tel: 21 342 6742. Open:
Mon-Sat 8pm–2am.*
Café Luso*
One of Lisbon's oldest
and most typical
restaurants and fado
houses.

*Travessia da Queimada,
10. Tel: 21 342 2281.
Open: Mon–Sat 8pm–3am.*

Timpanas*
Typical Portuguese
bacalhau and fish dishes,
and a good helping of
fado.
*Rua Gilberto Rala, 24.
Tel: 21 390 6655.
Open: Thur–Tue
8.30pm–2am.*

International
Bica do Sapato*
Trendy nouvelle cuisine
restaurant.
*Avenida Infante Dom
Henrique, Armazém B,
Cais da Pedra (Parque
das Nações). Tel: 21 881
0320. Open: daily
12.30–2.30pm &
8–11.30pm.*
Brasserie Avenue*
International menu with
a buffet during weekday
lunchtimes.

Snacks can be bought from street vendors

*Avenida da Liberdade,
127 (Hotel Sofitel).
Tel: 21 322 8350.
Open: daily 12.30–3pm
& 7.30–11pm.*
Buffalo Grill**
Riverside restaurant with
a Brazilian-style brasserie
or *rodizio*. Turn on the
'GO' sign for as long as
you can eat.
*Passeio das Tágides.
Tel: 21 892 2750.
Open: daily 12.30–3.30pm
& 7.30–11.30pm.*
**Café Martinho da
Arcada****
Portuguese and
international cuisine.

Popular with the arty
crowd and for business
lunches.
*Praça do Comércio, 3.
Tel: 21 886 6213. Open:
Mon–Sat 8am–10pm.*
Cervejaria Alma***
Serves German
specialities and beer,
steaks and shellfish.
*Rua do Ale rim, 23.
Tel: 21 342 2916. Open:
Mon–Sat 9–2am.*
Cosmos Café**
Mediterranean menu.
*Doca de Santo Amaro,
Armazém 5 (Alcântara).
Tel: 21 397 2747. Open:
daily 12.30pm–12.30am.*

Doca de Santo*
Good salads, snacks and
food at this large dockside
bar/restaurant with plenty
of room for the children.
*Open: Mon–Thur & Sun
12.30pm–1am, Fri–Sat
12.30pm–3am.*
Hennessy's Irish Pub*
Serves Portuguese cuisine
but has Irish dishes in the
evening, and live music.
*Rua do Cais do Sore.
Tel: 21 343 1064.
Open: Mon–Thur & Sun
noon–2am; Fri & Sat
12.30pm–3am.*
Outback Steakhouse**
Serves Australian and
American food.
*Rua da Cincture do
Porto de Lisboan,
Armazém 255, Santos.
Tel: 21 324 2910.*
Speakeasy**
This riverfront restaurant
has live music every night
from 11pm, but is
particularly busy at the
weekends.
*Cais Officinal, Roche
Coned Abides.
Tel: 21 396 4257. Open:
Tue–Thur 8pm–3am,
Fri & Sat 8pm–4am.*
Uai***
Brazilian cooking from
the state of Minas Geris.
*Roche do Coned de
Abides, Armazém 14
(by revolving bridge).
Tel: 21 390 0111. Open:*

Typical restaurant in the Ribeira, Porto

Pasteis de Nata – typical Portuguese custard tarts

Tue–Wed 8am–11pm,
Thur–Sat 12.30–3pm &
8–11pm.

PORTO RESTAURANTS
Portuguese Cuisine
Abadia*
Serves baked bacalhau
and its own style of tripe
and veal chops.
Rua Avenue Commercial,
22–4. Tel: 22 200 8757.
Open: daily noon–11pm.
Ateneu*
Cooks Braga-style bacalhau
and barbecued chicken.
Rua Avenue Commercial,
8–14. Tel: 22 200 4106.
Open: daily 9am–midnight.

Bonaparte**
Pub-style restaurant
serving meat, cheese
and chocolate fondues.
Avenida Brazil, 130.
Tel: 22 618 8404.
Open: daily 5pm–4am.
Cervejaria Galiza*
Steaks and seafood with
beer.
Rua do Campo Alegre, 55.
Tel: 22 608 4442. Open:
daily 8–1.45am.
Churrascão do Mar***
Has a superb fish menu
Rua João Grave 134/152.
Tel: 22 609 6382.
Open: Mon–Sat
noon–3.30pm/ 7–11pm.

Cufra*
Francesinhas and
house special seafood
stew and steaks.
Avenida da Boavista,
2504.
Tel: 22 617 2715.
Open: daily Tue–Sun
noon–2am.
D Filipa***
Serves good quality
Portuguese and
international food.
Hotel Infante de Sagres,
Praça D Filipa de
Lencastre, 62.
Tel: 22 339 8500.
Open: daily 12.30–2.30pm
& 7.30–10.30pm.

Don Manoel**
Oven-roasted kid and veal, as well as various kinds of fish.
Avenida Montevideu, 384. Tel: 22 617 2304. Open: Mon–Sat 12.30–5pm & 7.30pm–midnight (closed for 2 weeks in Aug).

Farol da Boa Nova*
Specialises in cod dishes from snacks to fishcakes and fillets. Also serves pork dishes and other seafood.
Muro dos Bacalhoeiros, 115. Tel: 22 200 6086. Open: Mon–Sat noon–3pm

& 7.30–11pm (closed mid-Aug–mid-Sept).

Filha da Mãe Preta*
Serves Mãe Preta's special cod recipe, seafood, pork and tripe dishes.
Cais da Ribeira, 40. Tel: 22 205 5515. Open: Mon–Sat noon–3pm & 6.30–10pm.

Francesinhas & Companhia
Serves the local 'toasted sandwich with gravy'. Definitely worth a try at least once.
Rua da Piedade, 33. Tel: 22 606 8136. Open: Tue–Fri noon–3pm & 7.30pm–2am, Sat 12.30–3.30pm & 7.30pm–2am, Sun 7.30pm–2am.

Madruga – Hotel Porto Palácio
Named after a local famous chef, the restaurant serves a mix of new and traditional dishes.
Avenida da Boavista, 1269. Tel: 22 608 6600. Open: daily 12.30–3.30pm & 7–11pm.

Mal Cozinhado***
Listen to some fado in the Ribeira while enjoying a slap-up meal of Portuguese delicacies.
Oiteirinho, 13. Tel: 22 208 1319. Open: Mon–Sat 8.30pm–1am.

Don't forget to try the Portuguese wine

O Fado***
A typical fado restaurant with live performances every day.
Largo São João Novo, 16. Tel: 22 200 0212. Open: Mon–Sat 8.30pm–1am.
Pátio da Mariquinhas
Live fado and typical Portuguese food.
Rua São Sebastião, 35. Tel: 22 205 7677.

International
Alfarroba*
Vegetarian restaurant.
Galerías Peninsular. Tel: 22 606 5286. Open: Sun–Fri noon–2.30pm & 7.30–10pm (closed Fri eve).
Brazil que Legal
This restaurant becomes a bar and late-night live music venue.
Rua do Monte Cativo, 426. Tel: 22 830 2758.
Chez Albert**
A selection of French dishes from coq au vin to crêpes.
Rua da Constituição, 1365. Tel 22 509 2318. Open: Mon–Thur 10am–3pm & 7pm–midnight, Fri–Sat 10am–3pm & 7pm–2am.
Chinês King Long*
Chinese restaurant with everything from duck to sweet and sour pork.
Largo Dr Tito Fontes, 115.

Tel: 22 205 3988. Open: daily noon–3pm & 7.30–11pm.
Churrascão Gaucho**
Typical Brazilian restaurant with plenty of meat and beans.
Avenida da Boavista, 313. Tel: 22 609 1738. Open: Mon–Sat noon–3pm & 7–11pm (closed in Aug).
Feito em Casa*
Brazilian restaurant that serves beans and grilled meats.
Rua de Cedofeita, 688. Tel: 22 200 3921. Open: Mon–Sat noon–3pm & 7pm–2am (closed in Aug).
Mendi**
Tandoori restaurant.
Avenida da Boavista, 1430. Tel: 22 609 1200. Open: daily noon–3pm & 7.30–10.30pm.
Pizzeria Meidin*
Pizza, pasta and ice cream.
Rua Santa Catarina, 949. Tel: 22 332 1922. Open: daily noon–11.30pm.

What to Drink
Portugal has 44 quality wine regions and, as markets open up, more Portuguese wine is finding its way on to the international market. For the main wine growing regions in Portugal

and Madeira, visit *www.winesofportugal.org/.*
Porto, of course, is renowned for its Port wine (*see pp122–3*) and no trip to the city is complete without paying a visit to one of the warehouses or sampling a few glasses of the fortified wine. However, there are several other wines in northern Portugal. One that is particularly unique is Vinho Verde, from the northwest. A fresh and light wine, sometimes slightly fizzy, it is perfect for summer drinking. For further information on brands, see *www.vinhoverde.pt/.* The Douro, Dão and Bairrada regions also produce quality wines.
Around Lisbon there are the Estremadura wine regions of Arruda, Alenquer, Torres, Abides, Alcobaca and Ecostas de Aire. Just to the south in the Alentejo region, there are some particularly good red wines, including Portalegre, Borba, Evora, Redondo and Moura.
Look out for Portugal's other famous fortified wines: Madeira, Moscatel de Setúbal and Carcavelos.

LISBON BARS

Bartis
This typical Bairro Alto bar still pulls in the intellectuals.
Rua Diário Notícias, 95–7. Tel: 21 342 4795. Open: daily 8pm–2am.

Capela (A)
This Bairro Alto bar inside an old chapel is a 'jazz sanctuary'.
Rua Atalaia, 45. Tel: 21 347 0072. Open: Mon–Sat 10pm–4am.

Cinearte
This nightspot is popular with personalities and plays music every Saturday night.
Largo Santos, 2. Tel: 21 396 5360. Open: Tue & Wed 1pm–1am, Thur–Sat 1pm–late.

Ginjinha do Rossio
Try the famous *ginjinha* at this tiny bar.
Largo São Domingos, 8. Open: daily 9am–10.30pm.

Lux Bar
Cool seventies retro bar popular with the 'in' crowd for late nights.
Avenida Infante D Henrique, Santa Apolonia. Tel: 21 8 404 977. Open: daily 6pm–7am

Piratis
Located by the Elevador da Glória, try the bartender's speciality of a blend of wines and soda.
Praça Restauradores, 15. Tel: 21 342 7869. Open: 9am–10.30pm. Closed Sun & public holidays.

Solar do Vinho do Porto
Stop at the Lisbon branch of the Solar and try some of the 300 varieties of the fortified wine.
Rua São Pedro de Alcântara, 45. Tel: 21 347 5707.

PORTO BARS

Aniki-Bobó
A now legendary bar, popular with the arty crowd.
Rua da Fonte Taurina 36. Tel: 22 332 4619.

Bar Homem do Leme
Waterfront bar on the esplanade in Foz. Have a cocktail while watching the sunset.
Avenida Montevideu. Tel: 22 618 1847.

Bonaparte
British-style bar in Foz that serves Guinness and Irish whiskey and has a restaurant.
Avenida Brasil, 128. Tel: 22 618 8404.

Está-se bem
Small and popular cheap beer venue, renowned for their house-special drink, the *traçadinho*.
Rua da Fonte Taurina, 70. Tel: 22 200 4249.

Labirinto
Nice modern bar near Boavista with a garden. Music ranges from jazz to house.
Rua Nova Santa Fatima, 334. Tel: 22 606 3665.

Pinguim Café
Another arty bar overlooking the Ribeira.
Rua de Belmonte, 67. Tel: 22 510 1474.

Pipa Velha
Rustic bar in the centre of Porto where you can drink wine and eat *chouriço*.
Rua das Oliveiras, 75. Tel: 22 208 2025.

Praia da Luz
Located by the water in Foz, this bar has a restaurant and regular DJs.
Avenida do Brasil, Praia da Luz. Tel: 22 617 3234.

Sobre as Ondas Bar
Great little bar located by the beach in Vila Nova de Gaia.
Avenida Beira Mar, 1661, Salgueiros Beach. Tel: 22 772 4293.

Solar do Vinho do Porto
The Porto branch of the Solar, again with 300 varieties of the fortified wine plus views over the Douro.
Rua de Entre-Quintas, alongside the Palácio de Cristal gardens. Tel: 22 609 4749.

Coffee and Cafés

There are thousands of cafés in Portugal, most with coffee high on the menu, closely followed by cakes and pastries. Virtually every street corner has a café or place to buy coffee, from the tiny street kiosks where you stop to down a *bica* or *café*, through traditional cafés adorned with elaborate décor and mirrors, to modern functional ones.

There are also numerous kinds of coffee. Most of the coffee itself comes from Brazil, Angola and Timor, freshly roasted each day and with a smoky flavour distinct to Portugal. It is served strong, in various forms: *uma bica* (small black coffee like an espresso) is the most popular. However, be careful because in Porto it is simply called *um café*; *café grande* is black coffee in a large cup; *café com leite* is coffee with milk (*meia de leite* in Porto); a small black coffee

with a drop of milk is *uma bica pingada* or *pingo*; and *um galão* is a milky coffee served in a tall glass. There are other variations according to whether the cup is hot or cold, whether you add hot or cold water or milk, amount of milk and size of cup. And if you want a decaffeinated coffee, ask for *descafeinado*.

You can drop in for a coffee and cake at any café, but to the Portuguese it means more than this. Cafés are a meeting point, a place where families and friends gather, and where people exchange ideas. You can spend anything from a few minutes to several hours pondering over your coffee, and no one will attempt to move you on.

Some cafés are legendary. In Lisbon, these mostly revolve around the artists, writers and philosophers who met at

cafés to discuss literary and artistic ideas and politics and philosophy. The most famous was probably Fernando Pessoa, Lisbon's favourite modern poet (*see pp62–3*) who frequented the Martinho da Arcada in the Praça do Comércio and, more famously, A Brasileira, in the Chiado. Here a bronze statue of the writer permanently sits outside the café drinking coffee in a pondering pose. While the Martinho da Arcada is now touristy, A Brasileira still brings in the locals. Every day at 10am a group of artists and writers continue the tradition by meeting at the table at the top of the stairs to discuss their ideas for a couple of hours.

Porto has its famous cafés too, used in the 1960s as meeting points for those involved in the production and promotion of the arts. However, these were renowned as more political groups, forces who opposed the dictatorship, reflecting both a general shift in public opinion and the city's long-standing history of political opposition. Unfortunately, many of these cafés, such as the Rialto, Primus and Brasileira, no longer exist. Others, however, including the Majestic in Rua de Santa Catarina, have now become institutions.

Facing page: The Portuguese love their coffee
This page – top: *Um galão* – a milky coffee
This page – above: There are cafés on every corner

Hotels and Accommodation

With rapid development in both Lisbon and Porto, there are a good selection of hotels and bed and breakfasts. They range from converted old monasteries and traditional hotels to modern state-of-the-art hotels and self-catering apartments.

Pensão Londres, Porto

Prices

Accommodation varies from basic (*) to standard (**) and luxury (***). Most prices include breakfast, but ask about this in advance because some more expensive hotels will charge extra. The better hotels have en-suite bathrooms, satellite television and parking facilities, but at the other end you can have a basic room and a shared shower down the hall. Breakfasts usually consist of a buffet service with a variety of breads, meat, cheese and cereals, coffee, tea and juices, depending on the hotel.

Location

In Lisbon there are excellent hotels located throughout the city, particularly in Praça do Rossio, Praça dos Restauradores, Avenida da Liberdade, the Praça Marquês de Pombal, alongside Parque Eduardo VII and now in Parque das Nações. The *pousadas* (*see opposite*) are located outside the city. At the resorts of Estoril and Cascais there are more hotels, including golf course hotels.

In Porto there are good hotels in the city centre and along Boavista, as well as on the riverfront, in Vila Nova de Gaia and further out by the sea. Again the *pousadas* are located outside the city. There are *residenciais* and *pensões* throughout the centre of both cities, usually in side streets and more traditional areas.

Americano Residencial, Lisbon

Metropole Hotel, Porto

Booking

You can book your hotel directly by telephone or through an agency. There are numerous websites which take bookings, including:
www.lisbonow.com/
www.maisturismo.pt/
portugal.nethotels.com/english/
default.htm
portugal-info.net/.

However, these online booking 'agencies' often add their own commission to the price, so it is often worthwhile booking directly.

Many hotels now have online booking facilities, but if you prefer to speak with them, most good hotels will have someone who can speak English.

The Lisbon and Porto tourist offices' websites both have a good list of hotels and other accommodation (*www.atl-turismolisboa.pt/guide/index_lodging.htm*;
www.portoturismo.pt/en/visitar_porto/onde_dormir/).

If you turn up in Lisbon or Porto without a reservation, the tourist offices at the airport and in the centre of the cities will be able to help you.

Pousadas**/***

Pousadas are state-owned accommodation and the first ones opened in the 1940s. They are generally considered to be quality accommodation and are either Historical Pousadas, located in National Monuments such as convents, castles and fortresses, or Regional Pousadas, located in areas of natural or historic beauty. There is a website (*www.pousadas.pt/*) where you can take your pick of the best accommodation according to taste and location. The site also has special offers, which usually includes discounts to the over 60s, and online booking facilities. Alternatively, you can call for a brochure and information at the reservation centre in Lisbon (*tel: 21 844 2001*) or contact your local Portuguese tourist office.

Modern Luxury Hotels***

There are various luxury hotels in Lisbon and Porto, both old and new. Numerous new luxury hotels have been built in both cities during the past 10–20 years. The older ones in Lisbon include the **Carlton Palace Hotel** (*tel: 21 361 5600. www.pestana.com*), **Ritz**

Four Seasons Hotel (*tel: 21 381 1400. www.fourseasons.com*) and the **Lapa Palace Hotel** (*tel: 21 394 9494. www.orient-expresshotels.com*). In Porto there is the **Porto Carlton Hotel** (*tel: 22 340 2300. www.pestana.com*), **Hotel Infante Sagres** (*tel: 22 3398 500. www.hotelinfantesagres.pt*).

In Lisbon, more modern hotels include **Hotel Altis** (*tel: 21 310 6000. www.hotel-altis.pt*), **Le Méridien Park Atlantic** (*tel: 21 381 8700. www.lemeridien-lisbon.com*), **Sheraton Lisboa Hotel and Towers** (*tel: 21 312 0000. www.sheraton.com*). Porto's modern hotels include **Hotel Ipanema Park** (*tel: 22 532 2100. www.ipanemaparkhotel.pt*) and the **Porto Palácio Hotel** (*tel: 22 608 6600. www.hotelportopalacio.com*).

A more traditional hotel in Lisbon

Pousada at Queluz

Other Hotels**

You don't have to pay through the nose to get a little luxury in Portugal. Apart from the *pousadas*, many hotels offer decent packages to tourists and business people. Lisbon's Heritage Hotels are reasonable (*tel: 21 321 8200. www.heritage.pt/*) as is **Hotel Mundial** (*tel: 21 884 2009*) and **Hotel Nacional** (*tel: 21 355 4433. www.hotel-nacional.com*). In Porto there is the **Grande Hotel do Porto** (*tel 22 207 6690. www.grandehotelporto.com*).

Resort Hotels*/***

Along the coast from both Lisbon and Porto there are several resort towns that have a wide choice of hotels, including ones by golf courses.

Residenciais **and** *Pensões* **(Small Hotels)***

Portugal has a wide range of small hotels that offer basic bed and breakfast. They vary in quality and location but are usually a great alternative to mainstream hotels.

Youth Hostels*

Pousadas de Juventude has a website that lists Youth Hostels throughout Portugal (*www.pousadasdejuventude.pt*) or you can telephone them (*tel: +351 707 20 30 30*). There are two hostels in Lisbon: Rua Andrade Corvo, 46, *tel: 21 353 2696* and Rua de Moscavide, 47, *tel: 21 892 0890*. In Porto there is one at Rua Paulo da Gama, 551, *tel: 22 617 7257*.

On Business

Portugal joined the EU in 1986 and was amongst the first member countries to adopt the Euro in 2001. Although foreign involvement in business has been prevalent in Porto's wine industry for centuries, since 1986 the country has opened up to foreign investment and companies. Membership of the EU has also meant further promotion of Portuguese business and products overseas. ICEP (Investimento, Comércio e Turismo) promotes business and tourism, offering support to both Portuguese and overseas business opportunities. (*For more information see www.portugalinbusiness.com/.*)

A businessman goes about his day

Business Hours

Most offices open 8.30am–3pm from Monday to Friday and close on public holidays. However, some businesses close at 1pm and reopen from 3–7pm. Banks generally open Monday to Friday 8.30am–3pm, but some in Lisbon are also open from Monday to Friday 6–11pm.

Conference Centres and Trade Fairs

Lisbon's principal trade and conference fairs are held at Feira Internacional de Lisboa (FIL) (*www.fil.pt*) in the Parque das Nações, where Expo '98 was hosted. Information on organising and attending fairs can be obtained from the Lisbon Convention Bureau (*Rua do Arsenal, 5. Tel: 21 031 2700*). There are also conference facilities at the Centro Cultural de Belém (*see pp40–1*).

In Porto, exhibitions are held at Exponor in Leça da Palmeira, Matosinhos (*www.exponor.pt/*) and also outside the city at Europarque in Santa Maria da Feira (*www.europarque.pt*).

More information can be obtained from the Porto Convention Bureau (*Avenida Inferior a Ponte Dom Luis I, 53. Tel: 22 332 6751. www.porto-convention-bureau.pt*).

Courier

DHL
Tel: 21 810 0099 (Lisbon); 22 999 0300 (Porto). www.dhl.pt/.
Express Style
Tel: 21 416 1682; www.expstyle.com.

Email/Facsimile/Telephone/Internet

The Lisbon Welcome Centre (*Loja 2–1°, 1–r/c, Praça do Comércio, Lisbon; tel: 21 031 2815 or Palácio Foz, Praça dos Restauradores, Lisbon; tel: 21 346 3314*) has Internet access, as do many major hotels, which also offer fax and telephone facilities. However, there are numerous Internet cafés around the city, including Café Peter (*Parque das Nações*) and Cyberbica (*Rua dos Duques de Bragança*) in the Chiado. Internet access

and telephones are available at the Portugal Telecom shop (*the northwest end of Praça do Rossio*).
In Porto, Cybercafés is located at *Rua Martíres da Liberdade, 223–5*.

Etiquette

Portuguese generally dress very smartly and so it is advisable to wear a suit when attending a meeting. You should shake hands with everyone present when you meet them and when you leave. Avoid pointing or being over-demonstrative.

While the Portuguese may not be on time for the meeting, aim to be punctual and call ahead if you know you are going to be late. Be patient as decisions can take several meetings.

It is better for foreign women to invite possible business partners to lunch rather than dinner. Business is never discussed at a social event and you should take a gift for the host if going to someone's house.

Money

The *Financial Times* can be obtained from most good newsagents along with the *International Herald and Tribune* and other major international dailies.

Office Supplies/Stationery

Most good bookstores have office supplies and stationery.

Photocopying

Major hotels offer photocopying facilities, as do business lounges at international airports. There are photocopy shops at all the major shopping centres.

Translation and Interpreting

Delta Língua offer translating and interpreting services (*tel: 21 371 2417. www.deltalingua.pt/*). The British Embassy in Lisbon will also provide a list of available interpreters and translators (*tel: 21 392 4000. www.uk-embassy.pt/consular/infogene/translators. shtml*).

Lisbon's modern International Exhibition Centre

Practical Guide

Arriving
Formalities
People from EU member countries require either a valid identity card or passport. Travellers from Canada, New Zealand and the USA only need a passport, but those from Australia and South Africa also need a visa.

By Air
Portugal's national airlines are TAP and Portugalia, but many major airlines fly here too.

Lisbon International Airport (*tel: 21 840 2060*) is located in the north of the city. The Aero Bus runs from the airport to Cais Sodré via Estação Entrecampos, Saldanha, Marquês Pombal, Avenida da Liberdade, Restauradores, Rossio and Praça do Comércio. There are also several local buses that stop right outside the airport, including No 44, which goes to Estação Oriente in Parque das Nações. If you prefer to take a taxi you must purchase a taxi voucher from the Lisbon Welcome Centre in Arrivals.

Francisco Sá Carneiro Airport (*tel: 22 941 2534*) is located about 20km (12.5 miles) northwest of Porto city centre. If you are hiring a car you enter the city via IC1. Because of the distance, taxis may be expensive. However, there is an Aero Bus, which connects the airport with the main hotels in the city and central Porto. For TAP (Air Portugal) passengers this service is free, but the fee for other passengers is reasonable. To return to the airport, book in advance via your hotel reception, the Mobility Shop or by calling *22 507 1054*.

By Ferry
There are numerous ferry routes on the River Tagus which take you from various terminals on the south side of the estuary to Belém, Cais do Sodré, Cais da Alfândega and Estação do Sul e Sueste.

By Rail
The Alfa-Pendular trains are a good way to travel between major cities in Portugal. They are clean, fast and reasonably priced. National and international timetables can be found at *www.cp.pt* or from mainline train stations.

By Road
Portugal is only bordered by Spain and the journey from one to the other can be made via motorways (AE), main roads (IP) and secondary roads (IC). You have to pay tolls on these roads.

Buses run to and from the airport

Camping

For information contact:

Parque de Campismo da Prelada,
Rua Monte dos Burgos, 4250–318 Porto.
Tel: 22 831 2616.

Lisboa Camping
Parque Florestal de Monsanto, Lisboa.
Tel: 21 762 3100.
Also see *www.roteiro-campista.pt/.*

Children

Children under the age of four travel
free on the trains, tram and metro and
those under 12 have a 50 per cent
discount.

Climate Chart

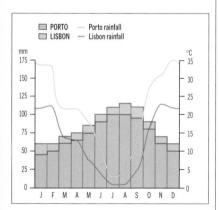

Conversion Chart

(*See p182*).

Crime

Although Portugal does not have a high
crime rate compared to some countries,
tourists are always targeted by
opportunists and there has been a rise
in violent crime in the past ten years.

Watch out for pickpockets on public
transport and in crowded tourist areas.
Tram No 28 in Lisbon is particularly
notorious for pickpockets and you
should be aware of your belongings
in the vicinity of São Bento Station
Porto.

If you do have to report a crime,
both cities have tourist police:
Lisbon, Praça dos Restauradores.
Tel: 21 342 1634.
Porto, Rua Clube dos Fenianos, 11.
Tel: 22 208 1833.

It is also advisable to keep a copy of
your passport in a separate place, along
with travel insurance details and
travellers cheques numbers.

Customs Regulations

Travellers over the age of 18 may
bring the following into the country
duty free: 200 cigarettes or 50 cigars
or 250g (9oz) of tobacco, 2l of wine
or 1l of spirits, 50g (1.75oz) of
perfume and 250ml of eau de toilette.
You can also bring in gifts up to the
value of €50.

However, you can still bring in these
items and more if the duty has already
been paid in any EU country. The same
applies when leaving the country. The
customs office is at Rua da Alfândega,
1149–006 Lisboa. *Tel: 21 886 81 85/21
886 83 61;* Rua Nova da Alfândega,
Porto. *Tel: (22) 340 3000.*

Driving

Portuguese driving can be rather erratic
and fast. There are one-way streets and
plenty of traffic jams. If you do not
follow the highway code, you can be
subject to on-the-spot fines.

Breakdown
Automóvel Clube de Portugal (ACP)
Tel: 21 942 5095 (south of Pombal);
Tel: 22 830 1127 (north of Pombal).

Car Hire
There are numerous car hire companies at both Lisbon and Porto airports. You can book online in advance from **Hertz** (*www.drive-portugal.com/*).

Documents and Insurance
Most driving licences are valid and you must have a licence for motorcycles over 50cc with valid insurance.

Fuel
Both leaded and unleaded petrol is available. Unleaded is *gasolina sem chumbo*. Diesel is *gáz líquido*.

Parking
Although there is some street parking, it is best to park in designated car parks, often underground. They are signposted by the 'P' sign and charge fees. Provision at shopping centres is good.

Traffic Regulations
You must drive on the right-hand side in Portugal. Seatbelts are obligatory in both front and rear seats, except for vehicles not originally fitted with rear seatbelts. It is illegal to have more than 0.5g of alcohol per litre of blood when driving and infringement can lead to heavy fines, arrest or suspension.

Electricity
The voltage in Portugal is 220 volts, so you will need an appropriate adapter and possibly a transformer.

Conversion Table

FROM	TO	MULTIPLY BY
Inches	Centimetres	2.54
Feet	Metres	0.3048
Yards	Metres	0.9144
Miles	Kilometres	1.6090
Acres	Hectares	0.4047
Gallons	Litres	4.5460
Ounces	Grams	28.35
Pounds	Grams	453.6
Pounds	Kilograms	0.4536
Tons	Tonnes	1.0160

To convert back, for example from centimetres to inches, divide by the number in the third column.

Men's Suits

UK	36	38	40	42	44	46	48
Rest of Europe	46	48	50	52	54	56	58
US	36	38	40	42	44	46	48

Dress Sizes

UK	8	10	12	14	16	18
France	36	38	40	42	44	46
Italy	38	40	42	44	46	48
Rest of Europe	34	36	38	40	42	44
US	6	8	10	12	14	16

Men's Shirts

UK	14	14.5	15	15.5	16	16.5	17
Rest of Europe	36	37	38	39/40	41	42	43
US	14	14.5	15	15.5	16	16.5	17

Men's Shoes

UK	7	7.5	8.5	9.5	10.5	11
Rest of Europe	41	42	43	44	45	46
US	8	8.5	9.5	10.5	11.5	12

Women's Shoes

UK	4.5	5	5.5	6	6.5	7
Rest of Europe	38	38	39	39	40	41
US	6	6.5	7	7.5	8	8.5

Embassies
Australia Avenida da Liberdade, 200, 2nd floor, Lisbon. *Tel: 21 310 1500.*
Canada Avenida da Liberdade, 198–200, 3rd floor, Lisbon. *Tel: 21 316 4600.*
UK Rua São Bernardo, 33, Lisbon. *Tel: 21 392 4000.* Out-of-hours emergencies *tel: 96 2720 560.*
USA Avenida das Forças Armadas, Lisbon. *Tel: 21 727 3300.* Out-of-hours emergencies *tel: 21 770 2222.*

Emergency Telephone Numbers
Chemist: *118*
Emergencies: *112*
General information: *118*
Tourist police:
See under **Police,** *p185.*
Car Breakdown:
Automóvel Clube de Portugal (ACP)
21 942 5095 (south of Pombal),
22 830 1127 (north of Pombal).

Health
Any public hospital can give you emergency treatment. Call 112 if you do not have anyone to take you, or in serious situations. You can also get advice and many medicines over the counter at chemists. British citizens can obtain an E111 form from the post office in the UK, which covers you for emergency care. However, it is advisable to obtain adequate travel insurance before you go.

Insurance
It is advisable to purchase travel insurance with adequate cover. Make sure you read the conditions and check to see if you are covered for any extreme sports if you are considering any. If you are hiring a car, check you have collision insurance and ensure the car you are driving is covered.

Lost Property
Lost property should be reported to the nearest GNR (Guardia Nacional de República – National Guard) station. The tourist police or tourist office can advise you of the nearest one.

Maps
Tourist maps are available from the tourist office, and more detailed maps or road maps can be purchased from most good bookshops.

There are several information points around both cities

Media

There are various English-language
newspapers in Portugal: *APN* (*Anglo-
Portuguese News*) and *The News*. These
can be bought at the larger newsstands.
There are various local newspapers, but
the main national daily is *Díario de
Noticias*. Other newspapers include
Correiro da Manhã and *O Público*. You can
also see world news on *www.bbc.co.uk* or
listen to the World Service, which changes
frequency according to the time of day
(*see www.bbc.co.uk/worldservice/schedules/
frequencies/eurwfreq.shtml*). Many hotel
televisions will have one, if not more,
English-language channel.

Euros are now the official currency

Money Matters

Portugal adopted the European Single
Currency, the euro, at the beginning of
2001. However, many places still list prices
in Escudos although you can no longer
use them as legal tender. Euros come in
seven different notes: 5, 10, 20, 50, 100,
200 and 500 euros; and eight coins: 1, 2, 5,
10, 20 and 50 cents, and 1 and 2 euros. All
coins have the same front throughout
Europe, but there are national symbols on
the back. You can use these coins in all
countries where the euro is used.

Changing Money

Banks generally open Monday to Friday
8.30am–3pm, but some in Lisbon are
also open from Monday to Friday
6–11pm. Money and travellers cheques
can be exchanged at banks and bureaus,
but they charge a commission. Bureaus
charge less commission, but offer worse
rates. Travellers cheques should be either
in US dollars, pounds sterling or euros,
but fees can be very high. You can also
use Eurocheques with a guarantee card
in some places. Withdrawing money
via ATMs (cashpoints) is now very
easy as most cards are accepted and the
instructions are multi-lingual. There are
ATMs and bureau de changes at both
Lisbon and Porto airports, and exchange
bureaus can be found in many hotels.
There are ATMs throughout both cities.

Thomas Cook travellers cheques free
you from the hazards of carrying large
amounts of cash, and in the event of
loss or theft can quickly be refunded.
Thomas Cook Travellers Cheque
Refund: 24-hour service – report loss or
theft within 24 hours. *Tel: 00 44 1733
318950 (reverse charges).*

You can transfer money using the
Moneygram service, *tel: 1-800-555-3133*
(from the US), *tel: 0800 897198* (from
the UK). *www.moneygram.com/.*
Diners Club: US *tel: +1 303 792 0629
(24 hours).*
MasterCard: *Tel: 21 315 9856.*
VISA: *Tel: +44 171 937-8091 (collect call).*

The Thomas Cook Worldwide Customer
promise offers free emergency assistance
at any Thomas Cook Network location

to travellers who have purchased their travel tickets at a Thomas Cook location. *Tel: +44 1733 294-451 (collect call).*

Credit Cards
Credit cards can be used to obtain cash advances at most banks and from the numerous ATMs. They are also widely accepted in shops and restaurants.
AmEx: stolen cards, *tel: 21 392 5757,* other, *tel: 21 315 5872.*

Opening Hours
Department Stores and Food Shops
Most shops open Monday to Friday 9am–1pm and 3–7pm, and on Saturday some shops only open from 9am–1pm. However, with the advent of large shopping centres, the shops are open from 10am–10pm seven days a week. Many supermarkets also stay open until 10pm.
Galleries and museums
Most museums are open Tuesday to Sunday from around 10am–5.30pm, closing from 12.30–2pm for lunch and all day on Monday. There are variations according to each museum.

Police
There are specific police stations that deal with tourist issues in both cities:
Lisbon, Praça dos Restauradores.
Tel: 21 342 1634.
Porto, Rua Clube dos Fenianos 11.
Tel: 22 208 1833.

Post Offices
Portuguese post offices are usually open Monday to Friday 9am–6pm, but main branches are open later and also on Saturday. As well as stamps they sell telephone cards.

Lisbon, Estação dos Restauradores, Praça dos Restauradores. Open: 8am–10pm. Estação do Aerporto 24/24 (open 24 hours a day).
Porto, Correios, Praça General Humberto Delgado.

Public Holidays
1 January New Year's Day
February Mardi Gras/Carnival (date varies)
March/April Easter (varies)
25 April Liberty Day
1 May Labour Day
10 June Portugal Day
14 June Corpus Christi
15 August Assumption
5 October Republic Day
1 November All Saints' Day
1 December Restoration (of Independence) Day
8 December Day of Our Lady
25 December Christmas Day

In addition each town/city has its own festivals (*see pp23 & 97*).

Public Transport
Public transport is relatively cheap and reliable. In Lisbon you can acquire a

Trams are an interesting way to see the city

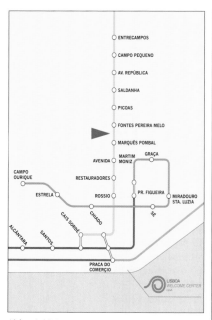

Lisbon's Metro

but you can change the time up to half an hour before departure. There are also local networks that connect you with smaller places close to each city. Timetables and prices can be found online at *www.cp.pt/* or directly from the station.

There is also a comprehensive network of coaches that runs between Portugal's major cities. There are various coach stations in Lisbon, but the main ones are at Arco do Cego on Avenida João Crisóstomo near Saldanha, at Campo Grande metro station (signposted) and alongside Oriente Station in Parque das Nações. For coaches going south towards the Setúbal Peninsular, head for the station at Praça de Espanha.

In Porto, the main coach station is in Praça da Galiza. There are booking offices at the station where you can obtain timetables and tickets. Some travel agents also sell coach tickets in advance.

Religious Worship
Portugal is predominantly a Roman Catholic country but there are also services for other denominations and faiths – consult the tourist office or English-language papers for listings.

Student and Youth Travel
Students with a USIT card and those under the age of 26 can get discounts on domestic and international transport. See *www.usitnow.com/*.

Telephones
Portuguese telephone numbers now have seven digits. If calling Lisbon or Porto from outside of the city you must add 21 or 22 respectively. There are

Lisbon Card for 24, 48 and 72 hours that gives you access to the metro and to the trams, lifts and buses for the whole period. Alternatively, there are various types of tickets and passes available (*see pp25–6*).

In Porto you can also buy one-day passes and longer from the Mobility Shop, or single tickets onboard the buses. The metro is currently being built (*see pp25–6 and p100*).

Outside Lisbon and Porto
The rail network connects Lisbon and Porto and the rest of the country. The Alfa/Pendular Intercity trains are fast and efficient and reasonably priced. You buy tickets in advance from the station,

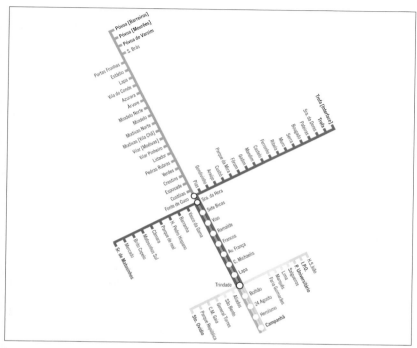

Porto's Metro

public telephones on the street, at the post office and in some Internet cafés. Telephone cards can be obtained from the post office, newsagents or kiosks.

Time

Portugal follows Greenwich Mean Time (GMT) during the winter months and between March and late September, GMT + 1 hour.

Tourist Information

There is a **Lisbon Visitor Centre** at the airport where you can obtain a taxi voucher and pick up brochures and hotel information. However, the main office is in the Praça do Comércio. As well as tourist information facilities, it has Internet access, a café and shop. There is another office and shop in the Palácio Foz in the Praça dos Restauradores.

The central **Porto Tourist Office** is located at Rua Clube dos Fenianos, 25. *Tel: 22 339 3472.* There is another office at Rua do Infante D Henrique, 63.

Travellers with Disabilities

There are toilet facilities, lifts on the Lisbon metro and ramps in modern buildings for the disabled, but access could be improved.

LANGUAGE

Portuguese has some similarities to Spanish and Italian, but there are many differences in both vocabulary and grammar, particularly with pronouns and definite and indefinite articles. Pronunciation is also different and if you learned your Portuguese in Brazil or Africa, you will have to adjust to the more guttural and nasal accent.

PRONUNCIATION

Stress depends on the ending of the word: stress is on the second to last syllable if the word ends in *a, e, o, m* (except *im, um* and the plural forms) or *s*; the stress is on the last syllable if the word ends in *i, u, im, um, n* or a consonant other than *m* or *s*; these stresses are sometimes overruled by an acute or circumflex accent over the letter, e.g. *é, â*.

Vowel Sounds

Courtesy of *Collins Portuguese Dictionary*:

a like the English **e** in furth**e**r.

ã like the **u** in s**u**ng.

e like the **i** in rabb**i**t.

-e barely pronounced, *arte* similar to **art.**

i like **ea** in m**ea**n.

o, ô like **o** in l**o**cal.

-o like **oo** in f**oo**t.

ó like **o** in r**o**ck.

u like **u** in r**u**le, but silent in *gue, gui, que* and *qui.*

Consonant Sounds

Courtesy of *Collins Portuguese Dictionary*:

Many consonants are pronounced as in English, except the following:

b softer between vowels, almost ha**v**e.

c before *a, o, u* as in **c**at.

ce, ci before *e* or *i* as in re**c**eive.

ç as in re**c**eive.

ch as in **sh**ock.

-d- softer between vowels as in **th**e.

g before *a, o* or *u* as in **g**ap.

ge, gi before *e* or *i* as in lei**s**ure.

gu usually as in **Gw**ent.

h always silent.

j as in lei**s**ure.

lh like **lli** in mi**lli**on.

m, n at end of syllable, previous vowel is nasal.

nh like **ni** in o**ni**on.

q before *e* or *i* as in **k**ick.

qu some words as in **qu**oits.

r-, rr similar to French **r** but varies regionally.

-r-, -r slightly trilled.

-s- between vowels as in ro**s**e.

-s-, -s as in **s**ugar.

-ss- as in bo**ss.**

z final **z** as in fla**sh**.

BASIC PHRASES

yes	sim
no	não
please	por favor
you're welcome	de nada
thank you	obrigado(a)
bon appetit	bom appetite
hello	hola (very informal)
goodbye	adeus
thank you	por favor
good morning	bom dia
good afternoon	boa tarde
good evening/ good night	boa noite
today	hoje
tomorrow	amanhã
yesterday	ontem
small	pequeno(a)
large	grande
cold	frio(a)
hot	quente
left	esquerda
right	direito
straight ahead	a direito
where is?	onde é
why?	porquê
what time is it?	que horas são?
when?	quando?
open	aberto(a)
closed	fechado(a)
how much?	quanto
expensive	caro
cheap	barato
near	perto
far	distante
day	dia
week	semana
month	mês
year	ano
do you have?	Tem...?
a table	Uma mesa
rooms free	quartos vagos

single room	quarto simple
double room	quarto duplo/de casal
bathroom	casa de banho
key	chave
breakfast	pequeno almoço
lunch	almoço
dinner	jantar
desculpe	excuse me (if you want
com Licença	someone to move out of the way)
Mr	senhor
Mrs	senhora
Do you speak English?	Fala ingles?
I don't speak Portuguese	Não falo português

NUMBERS

1	um(a)
2	dois (duas feminine)
3	três
4	cuatro
5	cinco
6	seis
7	sete
8	oito
9	nove
10	dez

DAYS OF THE WEEK

Sunday	domingo
Monday	segunda-feira
Tuesday	terça-feira
Wednesday	quarta-feira
Thursday	quinta-feira
Friday	sexta-feira
Saturday	sábado

ACKNOWLEDGEMENTS

Thomas Cook Publishing wishes to thank the photographers, picture libraries and other organisations for the loan of the photographs reproduced in this book, to whom the copyright in the photographs belong.

ACE STOCK spine

ARQUIVO FOTOGRÁFICO DO SANTUÁRIO DE FÁTIMA 77b

CÂMARA MUNICIPAL DE MATOSINHOS 159

CÂMARA MUNICIPAL DE PORTO 97

ICEP (PORTUGUESE TOURIST OFFICE) 82

LOUISE POLE-BAKER 48, 74, 75, 114b, 115, 158, 164

MARY POLE-BAKER 77a, 154

LUÍS OLIVEIRA SANTOS 93, 94a, 111, 134, 138a, 138b, 139, 151

TURISMO DE LISBON 157, 168

The remaining pictures were taken by NEIL SETCHFIELD including back cover photos.

Copy-editing: Joanne Osborn

Index: Indexing Specialists (UK) Ltd

Maps: IFA Design Ltd, Plymouth, UK

Proof-reading: Cambridge Publishing Management Ltd and Kevin Parnell

Travellers

Feedback Form

Please help us improve future editions by taking part in our reader survey. Every returned form will be acknowledged. To show our appreciation we will send you a voucher entitling you to £1 off your next *Travellers* guide or any other Thomas Cook guidebook ordered direct from Thomas Cook Publishing. Just take a few minutes to complete and return this form to us.

We'd also be glad to hear of your comments, updates or recommendations on places we cover or you think that we ought to cover.

1. Which *Travellers* guide did you purchase?

_____

2. Have you purchased other *Travellers* guides in the series?

    Yes   ☐

    No   ☐

    If Yes, please specify_____

3. Which of the following tempted you into buying your *Travellers* guide: (Please tick as many as appropriate)

    The price   ☐

    The FREE weblinks CD   ☐

    The cover   ☐

    The content   ☐

    Other_____

4. What do you think of :

    a) the cover design? _____

    b) the design and layout styles within the book?_____

    c) the FREE weblinks CD?_____

5. Please tell us about any features that in your opinion could be changed, improved or added in future editions of the book or CD:

_____

_____

Your age category: ☐ under 21 ☐ 21-30 ☐ 31-40 ☐ 41-50 ☐ 51+

Mr/Mrs/Miss/Ms/Other

Surname_____ Initials_____

Full address: (Please include postal or zip code)_____

_____

Daytime telephone number: _____

Email address:_____

☐ Please tick here if you would be willing to participate in further customer surveys.

☐ Please tick here if you would like to receive information on new titles or special offers from Thomas Cook Publishing (please note we never give your details to third party companies).

Please detach this page and send it to: **The Editor, Travellers, Thomas Cook Publishing, PO Box 227, The Thomas Cook Business Park, Peterborough PE3 8XX, United Kingdom.**

tear along the perforation

The Editor, Travellers
Thomas Cook Publishing
PO Box 227
The Thomas Cook Business Park
Peterborough, PE3 8XX
United Kingdom

Thomas Cook

Publishing